INFINITE IMPACT

The word *infinite* in the title of this book is used in its colloquial sense, meaning "without end" or "timeless." In theological parlance, the term is, of course, reserved exclusively for Deity. In this sense, God alone is absolute and infinite, without limit of any kind. As used in the title of this book, *infinite* is intended to describe the impact of an individual life outside the normal considerations of its beginning and ending in time. In this sense, the impact of a single life is indefinitely vast and extensive because of God's gracious invitation to join him in eternal, never-ending life. Therefore, what we do here and now echoes in eternity.

TYNDALE HOUSE PUBLISHERS, INC.
CAROL STREAM, ILLINOIS

INFINITE

IMPACT

Making the Most of Your Place on God's Timeline

STU WEBER

Visit Tyndale's exciting Web site at www.tyndale.com

TYNDALE and Tyndale's quill logo are registered trademarks of Tyndale House Publishers, Inc.

Infinite Impact: Making the Most of Your Place on God's Timeline

Copyright © 2007 by Stu Weber. All rights reserved.

Cover photo copyright © by PunchStock. All rights reserved.

Designed by Jacqueline L. Noe

Edited by Dave Lindstedt

Scripture quotations marked NLT are taken from the *Holy Bible,* New Living Translation, copyright © 1996, 2004. Used by permission of Tyndale House Publishers, Inc., Carol Stream, Illinois 60188. All rights reserved.

Scripture quotations marked NASB are taken from the *New American Standard Bible,* © 1960, 1962, 1963, 1968, 1971, 1972, 1973, 1975, 1977, 1995 by The Lockman Foundation. Used by permission.

Scripture quotations marked NIV are taken from the *Holy Bible,* New International Version®. NIV®. Copyright © 1973, 1978, 1984 by International Bible Society. Used by permission of Zondervan. All rights reserved.

Scripture quotations marked NKJV are taken from the New King James Version. Copyright © 1982 by Thomas Nelson, Inc. Used by permission. All rights reserved.

Scripture verses marked PHILLIPS are taken from *The New Testament in Modern English* by J. B. Phillips, copyright © J. B. Phillips, 1958, 1959, 1960, 1972. All rights reserved.

Scripture marked THE MESSAGE taken from *The Message.* Copyright © 1993, 1994, 1995, 1996, 2000, 2001, 2002. Used by permission of NavPress Publishing Group.

Scripture quotations marked AMP are taken from *The Amplified Bible.* Old Testament copyright © 1965, 1987 by The Zondervan Corporation. *The Amplified New Testament* copyright © 1958, 1987 by The Lockman Foundation. Used by permission.

Library of Congress Cataloging-in-Publication Data

Weber, Stu.
  Infinite impact : making the most of your place on God's timeline / Stu Weber.
    p. cm.
  Includes bibliographical references.
  ISBN-13: 978-0-8423-7441-5 (hc)
  ISBN-10: 0-8423-7441-8 (hc)
  ISBN-13: 978-0-8423-7442-2 (sc)
  ISBN-10: 0-8423-7442-6 (sc)
  1. Christian life. I. Title.
  BV4501.3.W395 2007
  248.4—dc22   2007020860

Printed in the United States of America

13 12 11 10 09 08 07
7 6 5 4 3 2 1

To Dad and Mom

BYRON C. AND DOROTHY M. WEBER

Thanks, Dad and Mom, for the memories and for the solid family stock.

To "our girls"

CAROLYN ANNA MAGDALENA (DRAKE) WEBER

JAMI LYN (COX) WEBER

JESSICA KRISTINE (LINHARES) WEBER

Thanks for loving our sons and nurturing our grandchildren.

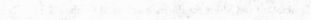

CONTENTS

ACKNOWLEDGMENTS

THANK YOU . . .

Randy Alcorn—dear friend for more than thirty years, for the gift of your heart, companionship, and encouragement; for your careful critique and wise coaching.

Larry Libby—friend, partner, and "consultant" extraordinaire, for your invaluable contribution to the writing of this book.

Joan Petersen—friend and personal secretary for more than twenty years, for your computer expertise, your filing, your footnoting, and for keeping me organized, informed, and on task. Mostly, Joan, thanks for your servant heart.

Mike Petersen—friend and churchman, for your computer expertise, for providing a place to write, and for bailing me out when the equipment caused me some consternation.

Dave Stout—friend and fellow soldier in the pastoring task, for thoughtful loyalty and coaching. Thanks, Dave, for your love for Christ and Scripture.

Steve Tucker—good friend for more than twenty years, for coming to my aid at a critical juncture with your excellent analytical skills.

Jami Lyn Weber—cherished daughter-in-law, committed family historian, and gifted writer, thanks for your heart and life.

Linda Weber—perhaps last alphabetically, but first in every other way, my faithful wife of nearly four decades. Almost forty years! We're both too young for that. Thanks, honey, for your consistent support and encouragement for this on-again, off-again project. Thanks especially for being so understanding in "shooing me off to write," even when it was inconvenient for "us."

The Tyndale team—special thanks to my new friends, people of integrity at every level, top to bottom.

SOMEWHERE AROUND THE TIME of that Harvard winter, I dreamed I was staying in a hotel. I had a wonderful room where all was well with me and I was at peace. Then I left the hotel for some reason, and when I returned, I tried to get the same room back again except that I did not know where it was in the hotel. If it had a number, I didn't remember it. The man at the desk said he knew exactly the room I meant. He said all I had to do was ask for it by name. Then he told me the name. He said the name of the room where I had been at peace was Remember.

I think of all the things you and I could remember that would not bring us peace at all, but I believe that at least part of what the dream meant was that way beyond all those things, at the innermost heart, at the farthest reach, of our remembering, there is peace. The secret place of the Most High is there. Eden is there, the still waters, the green pastures. Home is there.[1]

—FREDERICK BUECHNER

THE TIMELINE

Gollum thought he had the poor little hobbit cornered. After a series of unfortunate turns in his great adventure, the formerly respectable Mr. Bilbo Baggins of Bag End had arrived at the worst turn of all.

Miles under the roots of the Misty Mountains, deep in the entrails of an inky black cavern, standing on the shore of a vast subterranean lake, these two now-familiar characters of J. R. R. Tolkien were engaged in a high-stakes riddle contest. If Bilbo stumped Gollum, the hobbit was free to go, and Gollum would be obliged to show him the way out of the goblin-infested tunnel system. But if Gollum stumped Bilbo, the lost little adventurer would be invited to dinner—as the main course.

And Gollum was *very* hungry.

The pair jousted back and forth for some time, and the riddles became increasingly difficult. Finally, Gollum unleashed one of his best riddles, and poor Bilbo, conscious of his hungry opponent's slavering anticipation, was at his wit's end.

> This thing all things devours:
> Birds, beasts, trees, flowers;
> Gnaws iron, bites steel;
> Grinds hard stones to meal;
> Slays king, ruins town,
> And beats high mountain down.[1]

Totally flummoxed by this puzzler, and with growing panic gripping his throat, Bilbo could see Gollum's eyes—two pale green points—approaching in the dark. With his tongue cleaving to the roof of his mouth, it was all the little hobbit could do to squeak out, "Time! Time!"

What he wanted, of course, was more time to solve the riddle. But by pure luck, "time" was the *answer* to the riddle, and Gollum's dinner plans were dashed.

The truth is, time has always been a riddle—to which many have sought an answer. Philosophers through the ages have grappled with the concept of time.

What is it?

Does it actually exist?

Is it an invention of the human mind?

What are its properties?

Did it have a beginning?

Will it have an end?

Is there a past, present, and future—or only an eternal now?

Toward the end of the eighteenth century, a philosopher named Immanuel Kant suggested a subtle relationship between time and the human mind. He theorized that the mind structures our perceptions so that we know instinctively that time is like a mathematical line.

A line.

A *timeline.*

Maybe that's the best our finite minds can come up with to answer the ancient riddle. *Time is a line between two fixed points.* All of human history—in fact, the history of our planet—is inscribed on a single line with a definite beginning and a predetermined end. Augustine called it a one-way journey from Genesis to Judgment.

Time is not some abstract notion, of interest only to philosophers, physicists, and hobbits; you, too—if you are reading these words—have a vested interest in time.

This isn't philosophy, this is *life,* and your life is on the line. Simply because you exist, you are inseparably linked to the timeline. And so am I.

At the end of last year, I happened to catch a network sports special—one of those sports year-in-review programs that crop up in December. In one segment of the program, they showed clip after clip after clip of sports legends who had died during the past year. The piece seemed to go on and on. I was amazed that there were so many prominent athletes who had died during the past twelve months. Face after familiar face flashed across the screen, with brief action highlights of their sports exploits. Some had died in their seventies or eighties, and some had not yet reached their prime. Yankee pitcher Cory Lidle, for instance, had slammed his private plane into a fifty-story apartment building in Manhattan and had perished at the age of thirty-four.

Here were men and women, old and young, famous and forgotten, from across the sports spectrum, who had played various sports in various eras of the twentieth and early twenty-first centuries. Although they couldn't have known it, they all had one thing in common.

Their timelines all ended in a single year.

And so it was for an unlikely trio—C. S. Lewis, John F. Kennedy, and Aldous Huxley—who all stepped off the timeline on the very same day, November 22, 1963.

My stretch of the timeline began on June 30, 1945, and only God himself knows when it will end. At times, I thought I knew the answer; at times, it looked as if my timeline had played out and was about to end—far too early, from my perspective. But I'm still here.

Not long ago, my friend and fellow minister Gary Beikirch and I looked back and realized that our timelines had nearly ended during the same two-week period in 1970.

• • •

We were young then, and soldiers, as the saying goes. We didn't know it at the time, but a single two-week window—on the far side of the earth—would become a pivotal point in both of our lives.

We both thought we were going to die. And Gary almost did. But what began with the brain-rattling, heart-shocking horror of combat became the start of a journey to a new way of life for both of us. *The* way.

We were both Green Berets in our twenties, each stationed at a special forces camp in the Central Highlands of the Republic of Vietnam.

At the time Gary Beikirch served as a medic, attached to the A-Team at Dak Seang, A-245, I was the 5th Group intel operations officer attached, at the time, to Dak Pek, A-242. The two little jungle outposts stood astride the infiltration routes in the tri-border region where Vietnam, Laos, and Cambodia come together, just a couple of miles from the infamous Ho Chi Minh Trail. The two camps were only a few "clicks," or kilometers, apart, and what happened in or around one of them had a way of coming down on the other as well.

What we didn't know at midnight on April 1, 1970, would completely overwhelm us in the next few days. Two full regiments of the North Vietnamese Army, the 28th and 66th, had chosen our two Special Forces outposts as their next meal.

And that's when everything began to change.

I remember crouching in a muddy ditch as the onslaught began, pinned down and knowing full well that our positions could shortly be overrun. It could be only a matter of time, and everyone felt it.

Newly married and twenty-five years young, I remember thinking, *So this is it. This is the end of the line for me. How sad. I've hardly had a chance to live.*

Some distance away, at Dak Seang in the wee hours of April 1, Gary was thinking similar thoughts as the NVA attacked his little outpost with everything in their arsenal. Ripped out of his bunker by scores of incoming explosions, Gary grabbed some M3 medic kits and raced across the exposed slope toward the fighting positions. It was his responsibility to keep his A-Team and their Montagnard allies patched up medically so they could continue to fight. Love for one's fellow soldiers may be the deepest of loves. Facing death together produces a camaraderie that defies description.

Within the first fifteen minutes, every American on the scene was hit at least once. Soon the NVA were inside the wire; mortar fire impacted everywhere, and small arms fire intersected across the camp. Hit by shrapnel, Gary noticed his blood dripping before he sensed any pain. No time to fuss with it, though; people were dying around him. His training kicked in. Gary hugged one Montagnard out of shock, covering the man's sucking chest wounds. Amid the flying bullets, he dragged another wounded trooper to the relative safety of a bunker.

The concussion and shrapnel from an impacting mortar round kicked Gary in the back like a mule. He flew through the air and landed more than fifteen feet away. He remembers thinking at the time, *Hey, there's a Purple Heart. . . . This is it. I'm going to die right now.*

Hit again in the back, Gary's bruised spine left him temporarily without the use of his legs.

His fellow soldiers urged him to stay in the medical bunker because he couldn't walk, but Gary couldn't stay; his friends needed him. He talked his two faithful Montagnard assistants into carrying him. He remembers desperate hand-to-hand combat, continually treating wounds, and pulling men to safer places. Finally, with his uniform in shreds and his body bleeding from multiple wounds, Gary had to be dragged from the field himself. But he insisted on being carried *toward* the action, not away from it. If his timeline was about to end, and it seemed most likely it would, he wanted to die *in* the fight, with his fellow soldiers, not lying in some bunker.

As he tells it, to really live, you must almost die. For those who fight for it, life has a flavor that the protected will likely never know.

The next few hours and days on Gary's timeline tumble into a foggy blend in his mind. Years after the war, he likened the experience to dozens of isolated incidents imprinted on individual cards in a full deck. At times, the whole deck gets shuffled and dealt; at other times, it feels like fifty-two card pickup—the stream of events scattering rapidly from incident to incident, dodging their way around obstacles and explosions.

Amid the fog of war and the confusion of combat that day, soldier after soldier, friend and foe alike, stepped off the end of their timelines. By all rights, Gary's timeline should have ended that day as well. But it didn't. The Lord of time and eternity still had plans for Gary's life.

Over at Dak Pek, A-242, I, too, contemplated the end of my timeline. What had shortly before seemed a life of promise and prospect suddenly raveled and curled right in front of me, like a ribbon in a match flame.

But it wasn't my time, either. I came through that tight place, as I have come through others in the years since. I have learned to affirm, as King David did, "I trust in you, O LORD; I say, 'You are my God.' My times are in your hands."[2]

My portion of the timeline is in God's hands, as is yours. He marked its beginning, and he knows the precise second it will end. However long our lifespans—whether we die young or attain the years of Methuselah—we know that in comparison with human history, our lines aren't very long at all. If all of history were a mile, our segments would be little more than an inch—or maybe two. And what we choose to do with those two inches of the timeline shapes our destiny and the interlocking destinies of many, many other people.

THE MYSTERY OF TIME

Time is a mystery (as the esteemed Mr. Baggins learned, to his great discomfiture). We acknowledge it, speak of it, recognize that we are in it, organize our lives around it, and sense that we are swept along through the days and months and years of our lives by its current. But no one really understands what it's all about.

Albert Einstein, whose own two inches of the timeline began in 1879 and ended in 1955, opened entire new vistas in the ways we think about time. But far from answering the riddle, he added layer upon layer of additional mystery as he postulated transcendental links between time, energy, and matter.

Einstein didn't solve the puzzle; he plunged us further into its depths. A riddle, wrapped up in a mystery, inside an enigma, to borrow Winston Churchill's famous phrase. We acknowledge the complexity, but we cannot unravel it. Solomon affirmed that God "has made everything beautiful in its time. He has also set eternity in the hearts of men; yet they cannot fathom what God has done from beginning to end."[3]

The secrets of time belong to the one who created it, who set its limits and boundaries, and who has always existed above and outside of it. How does one explain that to the philosophers? The apostle Paul took a shot at it when he stood before the leading intellectual lights of Athens and declared, "From one man [God] made every nation of men, that they should inhabit the whole earth; *and he determined the times set for them* and the exact places where they should live."[4]

I especially like the words of Jesus on the subject of time: "Who of you by worrying can add a single hour to his life? Since you cannot do this *very little thing,* why do you worry about the rest?"[5]

Isn't that good? Adding an hour to our lives—or a day or a year—

is a "very little thing" to the Lord of time. He can do whatever he pleases with time—even *stop* it, as he did in answer to the direct prayer of one of his handpicked warriors (see Joshua 10:12-14).

Joshua didn't understand the physics of stopping the sun over Gibeon and the moon over the Valley of Aijalon for an extra twenty-four hours; he just knew he had a big job to do and an even bigger God who could do *anything*. So what's the problem?

No, we'll never be able to unravel all the mysteries of time. But we can gain wisdom in how we *use* time. That's what Moses is getting at in Psalm 90 when he prays, "Teach us to number our days aright, that we may gain a heart of wisdom."[6] Paul writes, "This is all the more urgent, for you know how late it is; time is running out. Wake up."[7]

The truth is, we can use time to our advantage. I'm not talking about "time management," but rather *time perspective*. We can learn how the timeline works and create a better future because of it. The Bible fairly brims with this kind of counsel, and the Holy Spirit will be our willing teacher.

In our culture of instant messaging and nanosecond-long searches of the entire World Wide Web, our perspective of time has been altered. But time itself hasn't changed. And neither has our progression along the timeline. When it comes to our own two inches of the timeline, we may be down to our last half inch, or we may just be getting started. Who can say? All I know is that if I'm down to my last half inch, I want it to be the finest, most joyous, most productive half inch of my life. How about you?

From his vantage point above and beyond the timeline, God has a perfect perspective on where we've been, where we are, and where, by his grace, we're going. I long to have God's perspective, don't you? Let's seek it together in the pages that follow.

PURPOSE AND POWER

If you accept the idea that we live out our earthly lives on a timeline, then this very moment—*right now*—is already part of the past. I hope you enjoyed it, because it's already gone by. You're further down the line than when you began this paragraph.

One philosopher pictured the passing succession of life's moments like a sizzling stick of dynamite, declaring, "The essence of nowness runs like fire along the fuse of time."

Sssssssssssssssssssssssssssssssssst! Look out. There it goes!

How fast is the fuse burning? C. S. Lewis described the future as "something which everyone reaches at the rate of sixty minutes an hour, whatever he does, whoever he is."[1]

Yes, it may seem as if time has slowed to a crawl as you sit passively in a chair or propped up in bed reading this book, but at this very moment your timeline is *on fire*—racing down the seconds, minutes, and hours toward its inevitable conclusion.

Before the advent of dynamite fuses, thoughtful men and women sought to capture the fleeting nature of time with other metaphors. Plato observed, "It is as if we were floating on a river, carried by the current past the manifold of events which is spread out timelessly on the bank." The apostle James was perhaps sitting by a river on a misty morning when he wrote, "You're nothing but a wisp of fog, catching a brief bit of sun before disappearing."[2]

That's a picture of the brevity of life as a whole, but it's also a snapshot of this very moment in time: a bit of fog, a flash of sun, and it's gone.

A melancholy thought? Well, yes and no. That's just the nature of things. We all know that life is racing by. Many of us are reminded anew every time we look in the mirror. But because we serve a God who is at once beyond time and outside of time, we can have confidence that the significance of our lives—in God's hands, according to his power and his sovereignty—can soar beyond all comprehension.

Peter reminds us: "Do not forget this one thing, dear friends: With the Lord a day is like a thousand years, and a thousand years are like a day."[3] In other words, a thousand years passing can register in heaven like the passing of the sun across the sky, from sunrise to sunset. *But it also means that a single day in God's hands can have a thousand years' worth of significance.* Little is much when God is in it, and every moment counts. God may not freeze-frame the sun and moon for us as he did for Joshua, but he can achieve precisely the same effect by expanding the reach and impact of each hour and moment of our lives.

But what of the moments gone by? What of the seasons we have already lived? Are they lost to us? It depends on our perspective. No, we cannot live them again, as much as we might like to (or shudder at the prospect). But remember, God is the Lord of our *entire* timelines. At the same "moment" he hovers over our present, he also walks in our past and goes before us into our futures. As David writes, "You go before me and follow me. You place your hand of blessing on my head."[4]

In this present moment, I walk with God step-by-step, enjoying his companionship. He has told me in no uncertain terms that the future is his concern, and although I may plan, dream, and prepare as best I can, I am not to worry (see Matthew 6:25-34; Luke 12:22-31). And my past?

Ah . . . glorious truth!

> You were dead because of your sins and because your sinful nature was not yet cut away. Then God made you alive with Christ, for he forgave all our sins. He canceled the record of the charges against us and took it away by nailing it to the cross.[5]

> "Come now, let's settle this," says the LORD. "Though your sins are like scarlet, I will make them as white as snow. Though they are red like crimson, I will make them as white as wool."[6]

God has wiped the slate clean of all our sin, blotting out all our betrayals and failures and selfish preoccupations, taking it all upon himself, releasing us from its penalty, and crying out on the cross to men, angels, and devils, *"Telestoi!" It is finished!*

Yes, he has taken away our sins, but he has not taken away the past. And though he will protect us from reliving the guilt and shame and regret of poorly invested days, he also has much to teach us from the past as we walk out the remaining quarter inches of our timelines. God possesses our past, just as he possesses our present and our future. In fact, if we do some looking back under his guidance, we will see things we've never seen before, truths that may directly apply to our present and our future.

Far from being a loss to us, the past seasons of our lives are often the means of our deliverance in the present and the very preparation we need to face the future. If you find yourself locked up, shut down, and paralyzed from taking action, the answer to the riddle may very well lie in your past.

What am I suggesting? Just this: I believe that God has left life-transforming secrets on the trail *behind* us. Your back trail—or mine. If you've ever read a Western by Louis L'Amour, you know that when his heroes traverse an unfamiliar stretch of wilderness, they will frequently stop their horses, turn around in the saddle, and study the trail behind them. Why? Because the land they just passed through doesn't look the same when viewed from the opposite direction. And if they ever have to find their way back, the terrain will seem unfamiliar unless they've seen the lay of the land, looking the other way.

> IF YOU FIND YOURSELF LOCKED UP, SHUT DOWN, AND PARALYZED FROM TAKING ACTION, THE ANSWER TO THE RIDDLE MAY VERY WELL LIE IN YOUR PAST.

It's the same with our lives. When the Holy Spirit shows us our back trails, we'll find landmarks and vistas we never even glanced at the first time through. The landscape appears different when we're looking back from the present.

I believe that God leaves treasure on our back trails.

GEMS IN THE DUST

A friend of mine recently shared a childhood memory of playing with his cousins out in an old apple orchard in southern Oregon. The boys were scuttling around in the dust when the eldest cousin suddenly bent down and picked up a twenty-dollar gold piece. Can you imagine that? How long had that gold coin been lying there, awaiting discovery? Very possibly since those gnarly old apple trees were seedlings.

What would it be like to find a gold coin or some precious stones along the path of life? A ruby, glinting blood red in the sun. A perfectly cut sapphire, blue fire flashing out of every facet. A five-carat diamond, catching daylight and throwing it back in a rainbow prism. Why should such things surprise us? We are sons and daughters of the Great King. Loving Father that he is, he wants us to live well. And no matter what you might think of your past life, the God who loves you has scattered priceless jewels of wisdom along the path *behind* you. Yes, there may be some bitterly unhappy memories back there and some dark passages you would rather forget. But what has God been doing while you've been living your life forward? He has gone behind you, and he has left treasure in the dust.

So, even if the past seems like just a bunch of dust in your memory, look for the gems. *You can apply the power of nurtured memories to shape your future.* I'm talking about the healthy sorting of memories—culling, and then discarding, the warped impact of the negative past; rediscovering, and then focusing on, the positive elements that have made you who you are.

> "EVERYONE WHO GOT WHERE HE IS HAD TO BEGIN WHERE HE WAS."
> — ROBERT LOUIS STEVENSON

Yes, we've all had negative experiences in the past. The question is whether we will allow those negatives to permanently eclipse our positive heritage. By reflecting on the positives, we can bless and redeem the past. By reclaiming our positive memories, strewn as they are in the dust of the timeline behind us, we can recapture their power to strengthen us for the timeline yet ahead.

I learned this lesson—or I should say was reminded of it—in the company of a three-year-old.

• • •

My grandson and I had spent the entire day together. Oh, it was a great adventure, and now we had come to the best part: Poppa and his buddy curled up on the couch together to watch a movie—and loving every wonderful minute of it. On this occasion, we'd just finished off the evening meal with a chocolate-covered ice cream bar. We licked our fingers, smacked our lips, and headed for the main feature: Disney's animated classic *The Lion King*.

As we settled into the couch, I noticed that my little buddy seemed to crowd especially close to my side and nestle under my arm. I said, "This must be a pretty scary movie, huh, buddy?"

All of a sudden a new personality emerged. His eyes lit up and doubled in size. His voice took on a sense of determined focus, and his hands and arms gestured with all the intensity a three-year-old can muster.

"Scar is a baaaaad lion!" He paused for a moment and then added, "And I'm gonna get my shaawtguun and shoot him when he shows up."

He scrambled for the ever-present pile of toys, looking for whatever it was he called his "shaawtguun." Unable to find anything that resembled one, he settled for a plastic golf club. The movie began.

You know the story. The kingdom around Pride Rock, ruled by the benevolent Mufasa, is blessed with abundant grass, sparkling streams, and healthy animals. The music is sweet. All is well. But Scar, the usurper, carries out his evil plot and murders Mufasa. Then he rids the kingdom of the young heir to the throne, Simba, by shaming him into believing that Mufasa's death was the young cub's fault. Believing himself to be a guilty prodigal, Simba wanders hopelessly into the far reaches of the wilderness.

And it gets worse. Scar's wicked tyranny systematically sucks the life out of the pridelands, and the kingdom devolves into misery. The once beautiful landscape is reduced to ashes. The water stagnates, the grass disappears, evil triumphs, and depression reigns.

And then . . . Simba comes to his senses. The entire story turns on a single scene, a scene that centers on just one word, one of the most powerful words in our language.

Remember.

On a starlit evening, Simba finds himself beside a pool of water. A refreshing pool of reflection and recollection. The pool of memory becomes something of an altar of remembrance, and the real Simba begins to emerge. Now full grown, but still in exile in the wilderness, the young lion has been encouraged by his childhood friend Nala to return and restore the kingdom to its former glory. But Simba refuses to return. Wallowing in the deep disappointment of his own past and its false guilt, he seems hopelessly lost.

In his disorientation, all he can do is stare into the pool at his own reflection. And then, in his reflection, he sees something larger than himself. Behind and above him, the pool reflects the stars sparkling in the dark. Voices from the past whisper on the wind, the familiar voices of the great lion kings of the past, repeatedly intoning one simple message to the young lion:

Remember who you are . . .

Remember who you are . . .

Remember . . .

Deeply moved, Simba begins to awaken to reality. He remembers who he is. He is Mufasa's cub, his father's son, heir to the throne. He begins to shed the dark side of his disappointing past and sees the brighter side of events that have shaped him. Starting, however hesitantly, to see the noble side of his father in himself, he hears his father's voice call out, "You have forgotten who you are, because you have forgotten me."

What is happening to Simba? It is the very same process that many of us need to experience.

At the pool of memory, Simba begins to realize that he is not just part of a meaningless animal herd wandering in a wilderness of forgetfulness. He has an identity. He is part of something larger than himself, standing on the shoulders of those who have gone before. A mantle has been passed to him, a just and righteous mantle.

Remembering transforms him from the inside out. Memory takes hold, and character emerges as the direction becomes clear. Simba resolves to return to Pride Rock and take back both his life and his rightful place. After defeating the tyrant Scar, he rebuilds the kingdom and restores the environment. The music is sweet again. All is well, and all because he *remembered*.

> "GOD'S CHIEF PURPOSE IN GIVING US MEMORY IS TO ENABLE US TO GO BACK IN TIME SO THAT IF WE DIDN'T PLAY THOSE ROLES RIGHT THE FIRST TIME ROUND, WE CAN STILL HAVE ANOTHER GO AT IT NOW."
> — FREDERICK BUECHNER

Frederick Buechner, one of my favorite writers, helps us to sort our memories when he writes, "I am inclined to believe that God's chief purpose in giving us memory is to enable us to go back in time so that if we didn't play those roles right the first time round, we can still have another go at it now. . . . Through the power that memory gives us of thinking, feeling, imagining our way back through time we can . . . [remove the power of the past] to hurt us and other people."[7]

Not only can we heal the wounds of the past, but we can harness the strengthening nature of the past to our own good and the good of those around us. By remembering, we can reform. By reflecting, we can bless the past. By reclaiming our positive memories, we can inherit their power to strengthen us for the future.

Memory is the lifeblood of character and identity. Forgetfulness is destructive. Remembering who we are is one of the most important things we can do as human beings.

THE YELLOW FORMICA TABLE

For Simba, it was a reflecting pool. For me, it was a yellow Formica table.

As I sat on the couch with my grandson as the closing credits rolled on the screen, my mind drifted toward my own past. The movie may have been over, but the impact of the evening on me was not. As my little grandson drowsed against my side, my mind scrolled through a recollection of my own—a memory more than half a century old.

When I was a little boy, I, too, spent a special day with my grandpa, William Weber. That day was also something of a great adventure, and it, too, had included the finest of desserts after dinner—one of my grandpa's famous ice cream and Pepsi floats.

Fifty years ago, there was no *Lion King*. In fact, there was no home video. Before television had become popular enough to start eroding the foundations of family life in America, my grandparents practiced an evening ritual of playing table games. As it turned out, that particular night, with a simple table game for our entertainment, would leave a permanent mark on my memory and my life. It was a memory that would also shape my future, because nearly twenty years later, the simple recollection of that night would save my career.

It's a story I've told many times, but I offer no apologies for repeating it here. *Life-shaping memories are made to be told and retold.*

Grandpa and Grandma and I were seated in the kitchen nook, at the old, yellow Formica table, playing Parcheesi. To my frustration, I had fallen well behind in the game, and I was becoming desperate. The last thing a scruffy little boy would ever want to do is lose to his own grandma. So I cheated. And I got caught.

> I WAS ON MY WAY TO BECOMING A CHEATER, BUT GRANDPA GAVE ME A VISION FOR A BETTER FUTURE.

The game stopped. So did the chatter. My grandma turned her eyes to my grandpa, and the mood in the kitchen turned very serious. I felt my face getting hot. Grandpa dropped his glasses down to the tip of his nose, and he looked directly into my eyes. "Stu," he said, "you're a Weber boy. And Weber boys don't lie, cheat, or steal."

I loved my grandpa, and I knew he loved me. His blue eyes sparkled, even into his eighties. He was a practical, straightforward man, and he taught me how to work with purpose. He was also a fun-loving man who taught me to laugh. I would never have intentionally disappointed him.

That night, he gave me something to live up to. I was on my way to becoming a cheater, but Grandpa gave me a vision for a better future. I had to decide. What kind of boy would I be? What kind of man would I become? Would I be a person of integrity, or would I drift, along with much of humanity, into a swamp of dishonesty, shading the truth, cutting corners, and trimming the facts to suit the needs of the moment?

On that unforgettable night in my childhood, that kitchen nook became something of a temple, a holy place. And the old Formica table became an altar. At the time, I certainly didn't understand all its momentous ramifications—mostly I just felt bad—but that evening became for me a life-governing memory. Twenty years later, when a superior officer in the Army directed me to falsify a report, I refused to lie. That night at the Formica table flashed through my mind, and I remembered my grandpa's words: "Weber boys don't lie, cheat, or steal."

Later, quite apart from any initiative on my part, the inevitable investigation (which deception always breeds) was launched. Not only was my own name clean, but the senior commander actually commended me.

Thanks, Grandpa. You gave me a vision for what I could be and a memory that shaped my future. *Nurtured memories serve as the baseline of our destinies.*

When my grandparents passed away, I was fortunate enough to come into possession of their yellow Formica table. That table is much more than something to hold food off the floor. It is a symbol of something much larger. Around that table, in our own little kitchen, Linda and I raised our three boys. Today, our youngest son and his wife have it in their possession. Together they're raising three more little Weber boys (as of this writing).

That humble little table, not much to look at in itself, has become something of a monument in our family. Think of it. Five generations have eaten at that table. Five generations have forged their characters and enjoyed each other's company around that simple piece of furniture. It has marked the timeline of everyone in the family.

THE STUFF OF LIFE

Memories are the stuff of which life is made. That's true personally, in a family, and in a nation. Elie Wiesel said it well: "Memory feeds a culture, nourishes hope, and makes a human, human."

Much like Simba, you and I have some pain to discard and some memories to nourish. For that to happen, we all need what Simba so desperately needed: reminders.

That's what this book is about. It's an opportunity to seek from the Lord of the timeline the invaluable gift he gives better than anyone else: perspective on our lives. As we walk through these pages together, I think you'll be encouraged to blow away like chaff those memories that would hold you back. I also believe you'll grab hold of the good seed, the healthy, life-bearing seed that is able to produce a family tree that will flourish for generations to come.

What we need are reminders that speak to us of who we really are, of what God has done for us, and of what our ultimate destinies will be. God in his grace, has, still does, and will continue to provide us with reminders—if only we will open our eyes, our ears, and most importantly, our hearts.

This we must do . . . for our own timelines and for the greater timeline that envelops us all.

YOUR JOURNEY ON THE TIMELINE

Impact Statement: Purpose and power flow from uncovering positive memories.

SUMMARY

- The young lion overcame his disorientation at the pool of remembrance.
- Memory is the lifeblood of character. Nurtured memories serve as the baseline of our destinies.
- The pool of reflection is a place for the healthy sorting of memories. It is learning from, culling, and then discarding the negative elements of our past. It is rediscovering the positive elements of who we are. It is harnessing our character for maximum impact.
- Life-shaping memories are made to be told and retold for our own good and for the benefit of others.
- Simple things, like Formica tables, can become monuments in our souls.
- Without a clear remembrance of the past, there is not a proper context for the present or the future.
- Memory loss destroys people, families, and nations.

KEY QUESTIONS

1. When was the last time you took a half day or more and sat beside your own pool of reflection? Will you resolve to do it soon?

2. Can you identify two or three negative memories you will choose to cull from your developing character?
3. Can you name, from your past, a person or two who has left a soul-shaping impact on you?
4. If you were to tell one story from your past, what would it be? Why?

MOVING FORWARD

Pick a day in the near future. Set it aside for yourself and your reflection. Write down one or two of the key positive memories of your past that continue to mark you to this day (even if it's just a paragraph or two).

2
STRENGTHENING
YOUR FUTURE

My friend Larry describes driving over the Mount Hood Highway one winter night from Portland to Central Oregon.

Larry had intended to get away earlier, but he was held up in a business meeting. Then, climbing into his rental car and heading east toward Highway 26, he was delayed by the Friday night traffic. By the time he was out of the city and heading into the foothills, darkness had already fallen.

Already hampered by poor night vision, Larry was additionally stressed by a maddening inability to figure out the high-beam setting on the rental car's headlights. Not that the high beams would have done much good that night.

As Larry began the steep part of the ascent over the pass, a misty fog settled over the mountain, reducing visibility to about three feet—or so he tells in the story. Even those conditions might have been bearable if he could have seen lines on the highway—any lines. But in the Pacific Northwest, the mountain roads are heavily sanded in the winter, effectively obliterating the center line and the line on the highway's shoulder. Just over that shoulder (wherever it was), Larry knew that sheer cliffs dropped untold hundreds of feet into deep canyons. He was afraid to go forward, because he couldn't see anything ahead. He was afraid to turn around, knowing he could back right off the cliff. And he was petrified to stop, for fear of the traffic coming up behind him.

So Larry prayed, confessing and reconfessing every sin he could remember. He promised the Lord . . . well, pretty much whatever the Lord wanted. Eventually, he did make it home safely to his family, but the sheer terror he had felt while hurtling through the night almost totally blind on a dangerous pass was vividly etched in his memory.

At times in our lives, on our individual portions of the timeline, we encounter similar foggy passes. We find ourselves moving too fast without really being certain of where we're headed. The night of sorrows and disappointments falls, and a fog of confusion settles over our souls. Where are the lines on the highway? Where is the side of the road? Where are the cliffs? How will we ever get to where we want to be?

Unfortunately, for about a half century now, the educational system in our nation has been systematically removing all the center lines, shoulder lines, and guardrails from the highway of life. We've taught our children that they have no roots, nothing to stand on. In fact, to add a grievous and fatal insult to their already injured souls, we have taught our children they have no inherent value. We've told them they've come from nowhere and are headed nowhere. They are driving in the dark, in the fog, with defective headlights and no lines on the highway.

Is it so very strange, then, that so many end up in the ditch? or over the cliff? My good friend Randy Alcorn describes most clearly what we have taught our children:

> You are the descendant of a tiny cell of primordial protoplasm that washed up on an ocean beach ten billion years ago. You are the blind and arbitrary product of time, chance, and natural forces. . . . You are a mere grab-bag of atomic particles . . . flying through lifeless space with no purpose, no direction, no control, and no destiny but final destruction. . . . In short, you came from nothing, you are going nowhere, and you will end your brief cosmic journey beneath six feet of dirt, where all that is you will become food for bacteria and rot with worms.[1]

Is it any wonder that our kids are adrift? Given such a dismal and meaningless foundation, should it be surprising that they would start shooting each other in their classrooms or simply abandon all hope and take their own young lives?

But the truth is that we're not merely the spawn of "primordial protoplasm"; we're creatures of infinite worth, designed in the image of the very God who created all things.

> From the moment of conception you and all other human beings are the special creation of a good and all powerful God. You are the climax of his creation, the magnum opus of the greatest artist in the universe. You are created in his image, with capacities to think, feel, and worship that set you above all other life forms. You differ from the animals not simply in degree, but in kind, in your very essence. . . . If you are willing to accept the free gift of salvation . . . your destiny is to live forever in a magnificent kingdom, to reign with Christ over the universe. You will forever enjoy the wonders of his presence and the marvels of his creations. You will spend eternity in intimate and joyful fellowship with your beloved Lord and your precious spiritual family.[2]

"When a society or a civilization perishes," writes Carl Sandburg, "one condition may always be found. They forgot where they came from." But if we understand rightly who we are as creatures made in the image of God, we will grasp two essential pieces of information for navigating the timeline we call *life:* We will know where we've come from and where we are going.

• • •

The arrival of spring in the northern climes invariably coincides with the return of the robins. And at our home, for the last three springs at least, there is yet an additional ritual performed by one of these red-breasted birds.

It's a robin . . . sort of. I mean, it looks like a robin, but this particular bird seems mentally challenged. Something's missing upstairs, or some wires got crossed in that little bird brain.

This is one robin that just never quite got it together. It flies, tilts its head, hops around on the grass, and looks almost normal. But there are three things this bird cannot do. It can't build a nest. It can't reproduce. And it has no song. No chirping on our window ledge.

For about two weeks each year, while the rest of the robins are mating and nesting, this poor, schizoid creature lands on our deck rail, stares curiously at its own image in the glass of our living room window, and then goes berserk. In what appears to be an attempt to mate with its reflected image, the bird repeatedly launches itself against the glass.

Thunk . . . thunk . . . thunk.

Occasionally, it takes a break and drags an odd twig or stray piece of meadow grass to the deck. It drapes the material over the rail— evidently its best attempt to build a nest. But like Narcissus of Greek mythology, this poor bird is learning the hard way that self-love is not much of a way to live.

That robin reminds me a bit of my generation.

In many respects, we baby boomers are the schizoid generation.

Disconnected. We never quite got it together. Oh, we look normal enough. We hold jobs, drive cars, and eat food. But there are some pretty basic things that we haven't done very well—such as building nests and raising our young. We have repeatedly launched ourselves into new endeavors, seeking an image of ourselves that isn't real.

It's been a mirage. And now that we're aging, we wonder what it is about life that still eludes us.

As a generation, we boomers have pretty much spoiled ourselves. As a group, we have no reference point for suffering or deprivation. We've known only the good times. We've made a lot of money, and we've spent even more, most of it on ourselves. Custom homes, luxury cars, exotic vacations, multiple partners, you name it. I sometimes call us the Cappuccino Generation: Lots of self-indulgence; little self-discipline.

> IN MANY RESPECTS, WE BABY BOOMERS ARE THE SCHIZOID GENERATION. DISCONNECTED. WE NEVER QUITE GOT IT TOGETHER.

We've spent most of our lives indulging ourselves, and now we're tired. Like that poor robin, we're beginning to realize that we can only "thunk" ourselves for so long before an awareness sets in that this isn't the way life was meant to be. Nothing ever comes of self-love. But we've been at it for so long that we've almost forgotten who we are.

We need to take a big lesson from that robin. At least it's doing one thing right. It's returning. It keeps coming back, every spring, as if it knows there's something here that holds the key to its life's direction.

• • •

Looking back, believe it or not, is actually becoming something of a national obsession.

On April 17, 2001, the official Ellis Island Web site opened (www. ellisisland.org). This database of America's ancestors, among them more than 22 million immigrants, experienced more than 450 million hits in its first three weeks! In the first six hours alone, it successfully served more than 8 million visitors. That is one of the largest Web debuts in history. And no one can say for certain how many millions of additional seekers were thwarted by the heavy traffic.

This example is just one piece of evidence of a snowballing trend: Americans are looking for their roots. Tracing family lines and searching for identity are hardly new pursuits. But current generations are pursuing the past with a new vengeance. And my generation seems to be leading the way. Fifty years ago, the unfettered future was all the rage. But today, trips back along the timeline have, refreshingly, become a growth industry.

> THE BOOMERS WERE RIGHT TO QUESTION AMERICA'S GROWING MATERIALISM, BUT IRONICALLY (AND PREDICTABLY), WE LATER BECAME THE MOST MATERIALISTIC GENERATION IN HISTORY.

Virtually all at once, heritage is everywhere. We see it in the news, at the movies, and in the marketplace. Hunting for our roots has become something of a national sport. Over the past two decades, backtracking along the timeline has emerged from a small preoccupation on the part of a few into a major popular crusade. Everything from Disneyland retro themes to the Holocaust Museum reflects a growing determination to rightfully engage the past.

Our parents gave us everything we wanted—and more. We had it all, including the money and education that allowed us to explore and experiment in whatever direction we chose. Of course, our parents were far from perfect. Many upheld the terrible practice of racial segregation, for instance. But rather than selectively critique the failings of that generation and bring about thoughtful reform, my generation threw out the proverbial baby with the bathwater. We protested, and soon discarded, virtually all our parents' values and lifestyles—the very lifeblood of our freedom.

The boomers were right to question America's growing materialism, but ironically (and predictably), we later became the most materialistic generation in history. We cut ourselves off from our roots, lost in our self-indulgence. Everything wrong with the planet was the fault of "the establishment," so everything that was established—including our history and heritage—was abandoned.

Today we are discovering that we have a deep hunger for the very things and places we once so eagerly left behind. We're beginning to realize the truth of one of the central dynamics of the timeline: The future can teach us nothing because it has yet to be realized. God certainly has the future in view, but we must progress along our timelines in order to experience it. The past, however, is accessible—and instructive far beyond what we have been willing to admit. We're finding that living without an awareness of our past is like being a single short chapter torn from a novel—lacking context, setting, and direction, too often without meaning or purpose, self-contained and yet incomplete. Individualism has turned us into pieces of a jigsaw puzzle. Our lives have some shape—and perhaps even an interesting shape—but because we don't see the larger picture, we can't know who we are or how we fit. We need to *share* a legacy in order to know how and where we belong.

In the end, we are all like the orphan consumed with learning his roots, like the adoptee who, even in the lap of luxury, is driven to leave it all behind to find her past, regardless of how poor, debased, or painful it might prove to be.

The Sikhs have a saying that I find quite apt: "If wealth is lost, nothing is lost. If health is lost, something is lost. If character is lost, much is lost. If heritage is lost, you are lost." Bottom line, we're looking to the past to find ourselves and to find a sense of place and identity.

RETURN OF THE NATIVES

Who are we? Where did we come from? How are we connected? Where do we go to find meaning? We're beginning to realize that the best place to find our roots is back home.

Like the famous swallows of San Juan Capistrano, we're heading home with an unerring internal drive. Like the Pacific Northwest salmon that traverse the mouth of the Columbia River each year, we may have been at sea for a long time, but we're returning to the waters of our birth.

And that is good. Very good. As Chuck Swindoll said so poignantly, "Home [is] where life makes up its mind."[3] Home is where you came into the world and where the world came at you. Home's lessons, like belted ammunition, are a series of rapid-fire first impressions coming at you one after another. And first impressions are lasting impressions. We are formed, shaped, and steeled for the rest of our lives at home, by home.

WE ARE FORMED, SHAPED, AND STEELED FOR THE REST OF OUR LIVES AT HOME, BY HOME.

There may be no clearer example of home's power to shape our futures as that of the life of General Tommy Franks, the commander of U.S. forces in the overwhelmingly swift invasion of Iraq in 2003. The defining memories of General Franks's childhood home went with him to the pinnacle of military power.

On March 19, 2003, General Franks, very much aware of the historic significance of the moment, heard these words via teleconference with the president of the United States: "For the sake of peace in the world and the security of our country, . . . and the freedom of the Iraqi people, execute Operation Iraqi Freedom. May God bless the troops."

In his memoir, *American Soldier*, General Franks describes the moment:

> The seven thousand miles separating me from the White House vanished. I felt the impact of the President's invocation.
>
> "Mr. President," I answered. "May God bless America."
>
> I saluted, and the Commander-in-Chief returned the salute. . . .
>
> I paused, climbing the stairs to my plane. The President had just ordered me to go to war. The troops were ready. The question in my mind was, *Am I ready?*[4]

Was he ready for the challenges he faced? Where would he go to find his answer to his question? Did he turn to his military training? to his experiences in Vietnam? Not so much. Mostly the general's mind went back home. To memories. He rehearsed the monuments in his own soul. Was he ready? Let him tell you in his own words:

> Strangely, I did not think of my seasoning in combat, my years as a commanding officer, or the military education I'd received in my career.
>
> Instead, my thoughts cast back to the small towns of the American Southwest where I'd grown up. It was this environment, my family, my friends, and my faith that had formed my values, my character. It was these elements that had made me who I was, years before I ever put on the uniform of a soldier. . . .
>
> My understanding of the world and its consequences— of right and wrong, good and evil—began when I was five in central Oklahoma.[5]

Indeed, life makes up its mind at home. Home sends us out onto the sea of life. And the tide of life has a way of bringing us back home again, whether spiritually and morally as in Tommy Franks's case, or physically, as in the case of George Dodd.

George grew up in the small town of Estacada, Oregon. After leaving home, he spent twenty-six years traveling the world as an electronics technician. But George is back home now—with a vengeance. "I never thought about returning to Oregon until I got older," he recently told a newspaper reporter. "I was having too much fun. . . . I guess when you face your own mortality, you start thinking about where you want to be and how you want to live. . . . I grew up spending time down on the river, picking berries, just being alert to nature. . . . You can't get that out of your system. That's what I return to."

Linda Johnson would agree. She came home, too, but not to the quiet countryside. Linda returned to the bustling city. After leaving home in the 1980s for Stanford University and a few years in Berlin involved in the arts and dance, Linda's back in Portland. She's still in the arts, but now she's nurturing the arts at home by bringing other artists and performances to town.

"It sounds very corny," she says, "but there's something about place. . . . I love living here. . . . I will be an old person here."

It's not corny at all; in fact, it's probably very wise.

Is it possible that our longings for home are part of being created in the image of God? I think so. The Bible indicates that God made us to enjoy a deep settledness—in our relationships with him and with one another.

One boomer recently described his wanderings and his weariness:

> While I steadily lost touch with my roots, paradoxically, I still longed for what was best about them. . . . Gradually, I became a multiple prodigal, internally and externally. A prodigal not just from a place; not just from a people. I wandered away in my soul as well . . . [yet] always longing to get back home. But I had lost the map to get there. The words of this old song described my struggle:
>
> *"Now the miles I put behind me*
> *Ain't as hard as the miles that lay ahead*
> *And it's way too late to listen to*
> *The words of wisdom that my daddy said.*
> *The straight and narrow path he showed me*
> *Turned into a thousand winding roads.*
> *My footsteps carry me away,*
> *But in my mind I'm always going home."*[6]

We boomers are indeed looking for rest for our souls. And we've begun to look over our shoulders at the timeline behind us—however reluctantly. We've begun to sort desperately through the "throwaways" of our youthful years, rummaging through the very things we discarded so arrogantly years ago. We've left behind the parties. We're running away from the materialistic rat race that we once rejected as a matter of principle, only to selfishly re-create later in life. And we're rather shocked by what we're finding.

We have discovered that the gnawing in our hearts is a hunger for the very things and places we abandoned on the timeline behind us. Finding that our inner longings are for the very stability we so soundly rejected, we're coming home—back to where memory, continuity, values, and history still live. Having thrashed through a wilderness of our own making, we boomers are returning to the trailhead in droves. And we're gradually rediscovering that real wisdom and virtue were not born with our generation.

Our returning feels good and right to us. It has the ring of truth.

> WE HAVE DISCOVERED THAT THE GNAWING IN OUR HEARTS IS A HUNGER FOR THE VERY THINGS AND PLACES WE ABANDONED ON THE TIMELINE BEHIND US.

ROOTS AND "PLACE"

Dick and Maureen both grew up in a high-desert town in eastern Oregon. He was strong and athletic, an All-American quarterback and student body president at the University of Oregon in the 1960s. She was quiet and studious. After college, they left the small-town life behind and spent twenty-five years in the fast lane in LA. The crowds, commuting, smog, and busy lifestyle left them unhappy.

"You don't have friends," Dick says. "You have acquaintances. I remember when it hit us; it took us six hours to get out of the Los Angeles city limits. . . . That was it. We had to get out."

Do you know where they went?

Back home.

"We make a third of the money we did in LA," Dick says, "but there's no comparison. We talked about moving home for so long, the romance of it. . . . It's great to be back home, where we know people. Grade school, high school, college friends. Where people care, where people stop and ask, 'How's your mom?' You can't get that sense of belonging anywhere else. Everything you do, who you are, it's all a part of it. . . . We can be who we are. . . . I can't tell you how glad we are to be home. We got our lives back."

George Suter went home too. And he also got his life back. He grew up on a farm that had been in the family since 1882. But George had plans beyond the farm. He couldn't wait to get moving, to see the world, to live a little. He built a fast-lane career as an airline pilot with a major carrier. Eventually, he added a coffee business with stores in Seattle and Portland.

But time changes things—particularly your values. Now George is back on the farm, and he couldn't be happier.

"The riches in life are realizing what you *don't* need. I hated [the business rat race] and what I call the ten-cent millionaires—there to impress, pursuing what they don't like, with things they don't need, with money they don't have. The realization of impressing others with ... jobs and possessions just wasn't what I wanted. It's good to come home. . . . You sleep with your window open . . . it's nicer, slower. It's quiet, spiritual, just doing the dishes or walking the creek. Being here has given us a renewed sense of faith."

Edgar Guest sensed the same thing nearly a century ago:

> It takes a heap o' living' in a house t' make it home,
> A heap o' sun an' shadder, an' ye sometimes have t' roam
> Afore ye really 'preciate the thing ye lef' behind,
> An' hunger fer 'em somehow—with 'em allus on yer mind.[7]

It's not just the boomers who feel these urges. We've all got it—that thirst for roots. The boomers busted, and now the busters are following the boomers home. And so are the generations coming after the busters. Most particularly, today's college generation appears to be far more conservatively minded than their boomer predecessors. They are beginning to reject the chaos and the revisionism of recent decades, instead seeking an identity deeply rooted in the authenticity of the timeline past. Even single-parent families (which quintupled in the 1990s alone) and unmarried couples (also growing in number) are joining the pilgrimage back home. People are longing to settle down, leave the rat race, run less, live more.

A HISTORY GAP

People need to know who they are and where they're headed. And the only way to learn these things is to know where they've come from. We can navigate for only so long in the night and fog with no lines on the highway. Sooner or later, the stress and strain will show itself.

Many of us are seeking those highway lines again—searching for an intensely personal "spiritual discovery." Anna Quindlen's *A Short Guide to a Happy Life* spent months atop the *New York Times* best-seller list. Claiming to help people "get a life," its sales swept the landscape like wildfire. So did *The Prayer of Jabez,* a concise little book based on a 2,500-year-old prayer recorded in Scripture. And Rick Warren's *The Purpose-Driven Life* has sold tens of millions of copies.

> WE'RE LOOKING FOR PURPOSE AND MEANING, AND WE'RE LOOKING TO PUT DOWN ROOTS THAT WILL LAST. WE'RE BOTH GRASPING AND GASPING FOR HERITAGE.

We're looking for purpose and meaning, and we're looking to put down roots that will last. We're both grasping and gasping for heritage.

Look around you. Genealogy and family tree software and Web sites continue to proliferate. Scrapbooking and photo preservation businesses, such as Creative Memories, are now part of a nationally syndicated cottage industry. And the word *popular* can now describe, of all things, history books! The books of Stephen Ambrose, David McCullough, and Jeff Shaara—all dealing with history—have made their way quickly onto the best seller lists.

And it's none too soon.

The Tonight Show often does a little segment called "Jay-walking," in which host Jay Leno interviews people on the street and asks them very simple questions. Many of the questions are about our history, common things that people ought to know. For instance, on one installment that I saw, he asked a young buster, "What did General Eisenhower do after World War II?"

With a blank look, the kid answered with a question of his own: "Retired?"

Dang. Missed it.

Jay gave him a follow-up question: "Did General Eisenhower, like, get a job after the war?"

The kid's face lit up like a lightbulb. This second question was now ringing something of a bell. "Oh, yeah, did he, like, make a movie or something?"

The kid felt as if he were hot on the right trail now, and he pushed it a step further: "Yeah, that's it, was it like a movie in black and white?"

Sociologists call that, bluntly, a "history gap."

One young adult, who turned thirty at the dawn of the twenty-first century, described what's been happening:

> When my grandfather was [thirty years old], he had lived
> through the Depression in the South, enlisted in the navy, and
> spent four years at war in the Pacific. . . . One of the first things
> he did when he returned home to Tennessee was to sire my
> father, who was born in July 1946. By the time [my father] hit
> thirty, he had watched the civil rights movement unfold around
> him and had fought in Vietnam, carrying a 12-gauge shotgun in
> search-and-destroy missions as part of the 4th Infantry Division
> in Pleiku. The toughest combat decision I've ever faced was
> whether to watch the networks or CNN cover the Gulf war.
> This is a fairly common story. People my age (and younger) face
> a history gap. . . . The problem is not our [un]willingness to be
> moved by events, or causes. We love to hug trees . . . or the series
> of "Ribbon Crises" . . . [but] the dangerous thing is that without
> epic scope, every news story becomes a "crisis," and heroes come
> cheap. . . . The cumulative effect of such confected moments—
> and the media's appetite for instant drama never helps—is to
> trivialize just about everything.[8]

Did you hear that? "Without *epic scope*"—the big picture—everything is trivialized. A broad perspective includes an awareness and knowledge of the timeline past. To find real meaning for today's circumstances, we must find our roots in the past. Context is the greatest indicator of meaning, and that's true with both language and people. To paraphrase Søren Kierkegaard: Though life must be lived forward, it can only be understood backward.

Some Americans are at least starting to get it. Though we, as a society, have seldom lingered in the past, many of us are beginning to stare longingly into the rearview mirror. We're beginning to ask ourselves some excellent questions, both personally and nationally. We can feel some of the unraveling in our cultural fabric, and we're beginning to see the value in our foundations.

Like kids in a neighborhood game of hide-and-seek, we're starting to run for home base. Only this isn't a game. It's life itself.

Your Journey on the Timeline

Impact Statement: Strengthen your future by linking to your past.

Summary

- Nothing much comes from self-love and pursuing our selfish "get-ahead" notions.
- Home is where life makes up its mind.
- "While I steadily lost touch with my roots, paradoxically, I still longed for what was best about them."
- Much of the hunger in our hearts is a gnawing for the very things and places we left behind. The harder we work and the more we travel, the more we wish to be at home.
- Returning to roots is a healthy practice, not only for swallows and salmon, but for people, too.
- People today suffer from a "history gap."
- Though life must be lived forward, it can only be understood backward.

KEY QUESTIONS

1. Is your life today so different from your childhood that there seems to be no connection between the two?
2. Have you ever had a hankering to revisit some of the memorable places and people of your past? Which ones?
3. Have you done so? Why or why not? Are they good reasons, or weak excuses?
4. Have you ever told yourself, "Someday I'm going to slow down"? Have you made *specific* plans for it?

MOVING FORWARD

Begin now, with pen, paper, and calendar, to plan a return visit to some of the people and places that have marked your life.

SPRINGBOARD TO ACTION

Aunt Ruth was my father's sister, and she was a wonderful person. Though the years dealt her some unfortunate blows, she was always a kind, caring, and hardworking woman who loved her family.

Then a day came when she didn't know them anymore.

She couldn't remember.

Ruth suffered from Alzheimer's—a disease that attacks the part of the brain most critical to the functions of memory.

My aunt's experience of the timeline changed, drastically. In the days before she was stricken, she ran life like a marathon, as all of us do. The course stretched out before her as far as she could see, and the miles fell steadily behind her. That's the way it is in a long race. Where you are is the sum of where you've been. As you reach for the next hilltop, as you stride toward the next bend in the road, your mind and body remember the steps that have gone before. There is context, and you pace yourself. You're not running a forty-yard dash; you're in the race for the long haul, and every mile you've covered is accumulated in the mile you're in.

It used to be like that for Aunt Ruth. But then the timeline became a treadmill. Life appeared from nowhere, immediately under her feet, only to disappear quickly, bending into darkness.

Alzheimer's disease starts slowly; its only early symptom is mild forgetfulness. Gradually, it progresses to the point that a person has trouble remembering recent events. Then the names of familiar things. Then the faces of familiar people. Before long, even the basic functions slip away—how to brush teeth, comb hair, get dressed, or find the bathroom.

WITHOUT A CLEAR REMEMBRANCE OF THE PAST, THERE IS NO PLACE FOR THE PRESENT (LET ALONE THE FUTURE) TO COME FROM.

And then, nothing is familiar at all. The person can no longer think clearly and has problems speaking and understanding. Eventually total care is required. Some regard Alzheimer's as a living death, for one simple reason—the person can't remember.

Without a clear remembrance of the past, there is no place for the present (let alone the future) to come from. Ask Nancy Reagan. In a segment of CBS's *60 Minutes,* the former first lady recounted some of the pain of President Reagan's final years.

"There were times," she said, "when I had to catch myself because I'd reach out and start to say, 'Honey, remember when . . . ?'" Mrs. Reagan described the pain of what should have been "the golden years when you can sit back, hopefully, and exchange memories, and that's the worst part . . . there's nobody to exchange memories with . . . and we had a lot of memories."[1]

Of course, a person who has lost his or her memory is still a person, but he or she is not the same person. If we lose everything that has shaped our lives, we cannot be the same. Memories make up most of what shapes us into the people we are. If we lose all knowledge of our past, how can we be the same person?

In the late stages of Alzheimer's, the patient has no memory. No history. No identifying recollection. In short, no self. It almost seems as if the person no longer exists. Remembering is essential to life and living. Without memory, we commit ourselves to a kind of living that is more like dying.

When presented in those terms, our memories—the good and the bad—are more precious than our most valued possessions.

What, then, of those with perfectly good minds who simply don't bother to think, to reflect, to remember? What of those who choose to live on a treadmill rather than run the good race?

They may be the saddest people of all, and most to be pitied.

● ● ●

"I shall remember the deeds of the LORD," writes the psalmist Asaph. "I will remember [His] wonders of old . . . and muse on [them] . . . teach them . . . and not forget the works of God."[2]

Memory.

Remembering.

God insisted on it; without it, man is helpless, a vagrant, vacant wanderer on the timeline.

In God's economy, remembering is undoubtedly one of the more potent principles. He insists on it from one end of the Bible to the other: Remember. Never forget. In the Old Testament books of the law, history, poetry, and prophets, and throughout the New Testament, the voice of the Almighty speaks to this priority again and again. "You must remember." It's as close to a mantra as anything in the Bible.

Virtually everything of spiritual importance or consequence depends on memory. Remembering is foundational, fundamental, and axiomatic. It might go without saying, but in failing to say it, we forget it. And in the forgetting, our souls shrink, our dreams wither, our hearts break, and Christ's kingdom suffers.

Memory loss is the most devastating spiritual toxin known to the human race. At least one member of the Trinity invests much of his divine energy simply combating our forgetfulness. Jesus said it straight up: "The Helper, the Holy Spirit, whom the Father will send in My name, He will teach you all things, and bring to your remembrance all that I said to you."[3]

Countless books and programs are available to teach you how to memorize the name of every person you meet. In the Bible, however, remembering is much more than a mind thing. Biblical remembering engages us at every level: mind, spirit, soul, and body. In God's economy, remembering means knowing, reflecting, and acting. It's all wrapped up in the same package.

Isaac Watts understood the singular power of memory to affect our human development. As I write these words, I have sitting before me a beautifully preserved 1798 edition of Watts's volume *The Improvement of the Mind*. The old English script is difficult for the modern eye to read, and the pages are somewhat fragile, but the truth is as relevant—no, *more* relevant—than this morning's newspaper.

> So necessary and so excellent a faculty is the memory of man, that all other abilities of the mind borrow from thence their beauty and perfection; for . . . in a word, there can be neither knowledge, nor arts, nor sciences without memory; nor can there be any improvement of mankind in virtue or morals . . . without the assistance and influence of this power. . . . It awakens the dullest spirits.[4]

In the Old Testament, the Hebrew words translated "memory," "remember," or "remembrance" are all related to a single root word: *zakar. Zakar* refers to the entire, multifaceted process: (1) mentally bringing something to mind, (2) the reflection inherent in that mindfulness, and (3) the corresponding behavioral act appropriate to that memory. In other words, to remember biblically is *to think, reflect,* and *act.*

I remember when one of my sons set out on a trip halfway around the world—completely beyond any supervision but his own. Prior to his departure for the overseas experience, we sat down in a restaurant together and rehearsed some of the dangers of young, single men traveling in places around the world where sexual mores are quite, shall we say, *loose*. The temptations are real—even intense. And sometimes faith must fight fiercely to win the day. We talked through all that. I told him about my own dad's faithfulness—to

> TO REMEMBER BIBLICALLY
> IS *TO THINK, REFLECT,*
> AND *ACT.*

his wife and to Christ—and how his model sustained me in some of the darker moments of temptation in my younger life.

About six months later, I received a letter from my son, making reference to our conversation in the restaurant, and containing these words:

> Dad, remember how you told me about Grandpa and your respect for him and your fear of letting him down while you were a young man overseas? How that memory of his faithfulness sustained you? Well, that's been completely transferrable, a hundred percent and then some. The grace of God—though not always because I've focused on it—has saved me thus far.

My son, like me, is grateful for his heritage and the memories of faithfulness. Correct remembrance prompts us to righteous actions.

To remember means "to hold onto" or "to trust." When you remember something, you call it to mind, believe and trust in what you remember, and order your actions in the light of that truth. To remember is to reflect, trust, and obey. Perhaps that's why the biblical verb "to remember" is most often used in the imperative. In other words, it isn't an option; it's a command.

God simply commands his people to "remember well what the LORD your God did."[5] To remember God is to live righteously before him.

GOD REMEMBERS

Remembering is central to God's very being, to who he is. He is the ultimate rememberer. Though we experience the timeline sequentially, as we've noted, God views it all at once. He doesn't have to "think back" to remember, because all of time is always before him.

With God, remembering means a good deal more than simply not forgetting. It's larger and more personal than that. God's remembering is actually a creative event—an action based on reflection. For example, "God remembered His covenant"[6] and went on to save and deliver his people. Or God "will remember their iniquity,"[7] and punishment for sin will inevitably follow.

> WHEN THE BIBLE SAYS THAT GOD "REMEMBERED HIS COVENANT," IT MEANS THAT HE DELIBERATELY CHOSE TO CALL HIS COVENANT TO THE FOREFRONT AND *ACT* IN COVENANT FAITHFULNESS TO DELIVER HIS PEOPLE.

When the Bible says that God "remembered His covenant," it means that he deliberately chose to call his covenant to the forefront and *act* in covenant faithfulness to deliver his people. When the Bible says that God will "remember their iniquity," it is to say that he will now *act* in meting out punishment.

God practices what he preaches, and for him, remembering and acting are one and the same.

Not surprisingly, therefore, God desires that remembering and acting become one and the same in our lives as well. Believers are, by definition, *rememberers*. The many New Testament commands to "remember" are usually calls to consider a particular truth or event and to identify with it so that our lives reflect it and our choices mirror it.

The Lord's Supper, for example, calls us to remember Christ's crucifixion and to affirm our identity with Jesus in his death and in his resurrection. We are to "conduct [ourselves] in a manner worthy of the gospel of Christ."[8] Our lives are to be lived in reflection of the price that Jesus paid for our righteousness. Our remembrance is who we are.

Ultimately, the eternal future of every human being depends on God's remembering. God's remembrance assumes either heaven or hell— hell because he remembers our sins accurately; or heaven because he remembers Christ's sacrifice and our names written in the Book of Life.[9] That book, which will be opened after the timeline reaches its terminus, is itself a memorial. It is a record of permanence, an unaltered memory.

No, God is not a revisionist. With God, truth is as it is. It is Satan who is the ultimate revisionist. It is the evil one who seeks to twist and warp the timeline past to his own ends, inspiring false remembrance. And when Satan (or anyone else for that matter) revises history, everybody loses. Revisionist history, based as it is on false remembrance, is absolutely destructive to the human soul.

Satan revised history in Eden by twisting God's words: "Did God really say . . . ?"[10] Eve couldn't seem to remember, and we're still experiencing the disaster. We *must* remember.

Satan even managed to lead disobedient Israel into revising their redemptive history. All it took was an appeal to human flesh—in this case the stomach—and history was out the window. "We remember the fish which we used to eat *free* in Egypt, the cucumbers and the melons and the leeks and the onions and the garlic."[11] Incredible! The horrible bondage of four hundred years of slavery was falsely remembered as *freedom*! Historical revisionism will kill you.

What are the guiding principles that give us proper perspective in our memories? Meditating on God's Word gives us the best things to recall—and a perspective on everything else we are to remember. If our own subjective opinions and personal dogma are our guiding principles, we would be better off forgetting.

> MEDITATING ON GOD'S WORD GIVES US THE BEST THINGS TO RECALL—AND A PERSPECTIVE ON EVERYTHING ELSE WE ARE TO REMEMBER.

FAMILIES IN THE BALANCE

Your family's future depends on remembering the past accurately. "Remember the days of old, consider the years of all generations. Ask your father, and he will inform you, your elders, and they will tell you."[12]

This great verse foreshadows at least two problems in the church today. First, the church is full of fathers and elders who don't know redemptive history. Many don't know the great Bible stories for themselves, let alone have a clue as to their intended meaning. Second, many of those who do know the biblical truths fail to pass them along to the next generation, leaving them biblical illiterates.

This verse is a call to family devotions, to catechisms, to Q&A sessions, and to storytelling. It's a call to conversations that should happen "when you sit in your house and when you walk by the way and when you lie down and when you rise up."[13] Contemporary families, however, seldom seem to figure this out on their own, which is all the more reason for the church to train people how to meditate on the things that matter most, the very words of God.

One Sunday school teacher in a strong evangelical church told me the results of a Bible quiz she'd given to her fifth graders, virtually all of whom were from "solid" church families. The sad reality? Only one of the students could name Solomon's dad.

What's the lesson to be learned? You can't pass along what you don't remember. And if you spend your mornings at the gym, your evenings watching sitcoms, and your weekends on the golf course, you won't know the great works of God recorded in Scripture. Further, you won't be able to see the great works that God is doing in your family and in the world today. You will end up conformed to the image of the sitcoms and talk shows and Hollywood, not Christ, leaving you with little to offer your children beyond affection and physical safety. In terms of protecting them from the world, the flesh, and the devil—the real enemies of their souls—you will be a neglectful, even abusive, parent, no matter if you manage to win a "Mom or Dad of the Year" award because you always drive them to soccer and volleyball practice.

You must remember.

You must remember the things that matter.

FROM THE ANCIENT WORLD TO YOURS

As you might anticipate, many of the things most worth remembering are the furthest back on the timeline. It stands to reason that the elements of living that have passed the test of time will be the most memorable. We modernists (let alone postmodernists) have a tendency to assume that unless something was discovered very recently, and within our own limited frames of reference, it can be of little value.

But that's not true. In fact, the opposite is true.

Consider, for example, the Scriptures themselves. Absolutely truthful and completely changeless, from cover to cover, across cultures and millennia, the Word of God consists of "ancient words, ever true" that still very much govern our contemporary world.[14] In fact, did you know that an ancient memory is still shaping the future of the twenty-first century?

> WE HAVE A TENDENCY TO ASSUME THAT UNLESS SOMETHING WAS DISCOVERED VERY RECENTLY, AND WITHIN OUR OWN LIMITED FRAMES OF REFERENCE, IT CAN BE OF LITTLE VALUE.

Few things in the modern world are more gripping than the role of the Middle East in world affairs. Our current century opened with world attention riveted on terrorism. We were overwhelmed with the events of 9-11. The hunt for Osama bin Laden in Afghanistan was the stuff of daily conversation. We were consumed with Operation Iraqi Freedom and its long aftermath.

Peace in the Middle East—or more specifically, the lack of peace—surfaces in some form virtually every week of our lives. The Arab-Israeli conflict, and its extension to the whole world in the global war on terror, is rooted far, far back on the timeline.

One of the questions that began to circulate in the aftermath of 9-11 strikes at the very heart of the issue of terrorism, radical Islam, and Western society: Why do they hate us so?

The answer, while not hard to discern, is difficult for some to swallow. Bottom-line, historic Islam is fundamentally hostile to any other religion or worldview, particularly Judaism and Christianity. What's more, that hostility began long, long ago . . . but in a galaxy not so far away.

The problems in the Middle East date from the time of Abraham, when his wife, Sarah, impatient with her inability to conceive her promised child and apparently failing to remember God's actual promise, took matters into her own hands. She persuaded her equally forgetful husband to take their servant girl, Hagar, and conceive a child to be his heir.

Abraham and Sarah's failure to accurately remember God's promise resulted in the birth of Ishmael. Moses, under the inspiration of the Spirit of God, summarizes Ishmael's story and his character with these words: "He will be a wild donkey of a man; his hand will be against everyone and everyone's hand against him, and he will live in hostility toward all his brothers."[15] That last phrase, translated here as "he will live in hostility," can be translated literally as "he shall live *in the face of* all his brothers." Does that not describe the current situation in the Middle East? It should come as no surprise that Muhammad, the founder of Islam, traced his ancestry directly back to Ishmael, the son of Abraham and Hagar. The point, though at times historically complex, is theologically straightforward: The past is governing the present and the future. That's how the timeline works.

AN ANCIENT WRESTLING MATCH

God insists that his people remember *accurately*, never forgetting his ways or his dealings with them. One of the most colorful Old Testament characters learned this lesson the hard way, in a wrestling match with God. By the time it was over, he was left with a painful *reminder* that would dog him every step of the rest of his life.[16]

God gave Jacob a limp he would never forget. To this day, more than 3,500 years later, the memories of that celestial wrestling match have stretched across scores of generations. That remarkable incident, as you might guess, centered on significant spiritual and moral principles. It featured God's presence, it involved the yielding of human will, and it contributed to the establishment of Jacob's character and personal identity.

Old Jacob, in keeping with his lifelong pattern, was having a rough go. His character seemed to be continually wavering in the balance. His whole life had been a struggle of one kind or another with his father, his brother, his father-in-law, and now with God. He was certainly known to be a schemer, a deceiver, and even a usurper. It was in his very name. Jacob was a supplanting "grasper" from the womb. That was his basic identity for a long time. But that began to change on the most unforgettable night of his life, when Jacob wrestled with God and received a memorable crippling and a new name: Israel ("he who strives with God"). It was something he could never forget, and it forged the blessing he would pass along to his sons.

Do your children know the milestones on your spiritual timeline? Have you told them about those moments when God spoke to you, rescued you, disciplined you, or miraculously provided for you? Perhaps, as with Jacob, you have a scar or two to show them. Your family needs to see those crucial intersections on your timeline past when God clearly moved in your life.

Though I've never wrestled with an angel, I've wrestled with a spirit—my own and God's. And though I did not pick up a limp, I do have a scar or two to remind me of those encounters.

> DO YOUR CHILDREN KNOW THE MILESTONES ON YOUR SPIRITUAL TIMELINE? HAVE YOU TOLD THEM ABOUT THOSE MOMENTS WHEN GOD SPOKE TO YOU, RESCUED YOU, DISCIPLINED YOU, OR MIRACULOUSLY PROVIDED FOR YOU?

My life, probably much like yours, seems to turn on several key pivot points. Vietnam will always be one of the big ones for me. Bombs, bullets, and booby traps have a way of marking a guy. Times of intense pressure and fear stay with us for a long time. And though I don't dwell on the details, I do make regular conversational reference to some of the crucial moments, the major intersections.

Like the siege of Dak Pek in April 1970 that I mentioned earlier. It's a year and a month and a memory that God has used as a fulcrum to shift some things in my soul. My grandchildren are too young yet for those stories, but my wife and sons know them.

I anticipate the day in a wrestling match with one of my grandsons when one of the kids will discover the small deformity where my rib was separated from my sternum. The inevitable question will take us back to the spring of 1970, and we'll eventually wind up at Dak Pek. I'll have the privilege and responsibility of telling another generation of the time God spoke to me, rescued me, and set me on a new course—a life of ministry.

YOUR NUMBER ONE WORKOUT

Remembering is possibly the most important exercise you will ever practice. It's so much more critical than sit-ups or jogging. Physical discipline "is only of little profit," but spiritual discipline "holds promise for the present life and also for the life to come."[17]

God apparently believes that it's important for us to remember our spiritual milestones. When he struck Jacob's hip with a lifelong limp, he was saying as much: "Every step you take for the rest of your life you must remember this night. You must never forget your dependence on me."

Remembering is essential in life; it's a crucial part of our identities and a key component of our personhood. If we simply drift along through life, neglecting to develop the discipline and skills to strengthen our remembering, we relegate ourselves to a kind of living death.

Remembering is one of the most important skills we can develop. In today's fast-paced world, we've lost sight of the wisdom that comes with age. For many in our society, it seems the past has become irrelevant, and they see no value in silver hair. If something wasn't invented or discovered in the last ten minutes or so, it's already obsolete, or well on its way.

The truth is, however, that most of life's greatest realities don't have to be discovered; they only have to be remembered. Some things never change, and truth is one of those things. In fact, the most foundational elements of life are those that have stood the test of time, down through the centuries. The currents of time, space, and energy may flow at breakneck speeds. But like great unyielding granite monoliths, the enduring principles of life stand fast. They're anchor points on the timeline, monuments in the human soul.

Memory loss destroys human beings at every level—as individuals, as families, and as nations. Loss of memory causes an individual to disintegrate. Failure to remember certain key commitments will cause a family to die.

Moses repeatedly emphasized the importance of remembrance, referring to it many times in the course of a single chapter: "You shall remember all the way which the LORD your God has led you . . . beware that you do not forget . . . you shall remember the LORD your God . . . [and] it shall come about if you ever forget . . . you will surely perish."[18]

The psalmist Asaph joins the same chorus: "Remember the deeds of the LORD . . . remember [His] wonders of old . . . muse on [His] deeds . . . teach them . . . not [to] forget the works of God."[19]

The prophet Jeremiah offers this poignant counsel to any who will listen: "'Stand by the ways and see and ask for the ancient paths, where the good way is, and walk in it; and you will find rest for your souls.'"[20]

> MEMORY LOSS DESTROYS HUMAN BEINGS AT EVERY LEVEL—AS INDIVIDUALS, AS FAMILIES, AND AS NATIONS.

We moderns and postmoderns tend to think that ours is the day of enlightenment and advancement, and that the ancients have little or nothing to offer us. One of the buzzwords on the political scene today is *progressive*. You are progressive if you abandon all standards, morals, and connections with previous generations. After all (we tell ourselves), science and technology have placed us head and shoulders above our predecessors.

That may be true, in terms of sheer data or raw knowledge. But what we're missing today is wisdom. We're missing the mature discernment that comes only from time, experience, and applied reflection. Our Creator affirms that there is no substitute for wisdom. You can't instant message it on your computer. You can't absorb it running from place to place with a cell phone clipped to your ear. You can't download it from a Google search on the Web. It comes only from time, experience, and applied reflection.

David learned some tremendous lessons about reflection and meditation during his years of solitude as a shepherd boy and later as a man on the run through a dry and desolate wilderness. "Blessed is the man," he writes, "[whose] delight is in the law of the LORD, . . . on his law he meditates day and night. He is like a tree planted by streams of water, which yields its fruit in season."[21]

A human lifetime, by definition, lacks enough experience for any real self-confidence. Being finite creatures of the timeline, with a beginning and an ending, we must rely on others outside ourselves.

In the book of Job, one of Job's insufferable "counselors" comes close to the truth when he affirms that men are too shortsighted and that the ultimate test of truth and wisdom is its ability to stand up to scrutiny over time: "Just ask the previous generation. Pay attention to the experience of our ancestors. For we were born but yesterday and know nothing. Our days on earth are as fleeting as a shadow. But those who came before us will teach you. They will teach you the wisdom of old."[22]

Remember the past and learn from it. If you don't, you're likely to walk blindly in the things that matter most.

> REMEMBER THE PAST AND LEARN FROM IT. IF YOU DON'T, YOU'RE LIKELY TO WALK BLINDLY IN THE THINGS THAT MATTER MOST.

WE NEED REMINDERS

We are physical people living in a physical world. God knows this. "He knows how we are formed, he remembers that we are dust."[23] In consequence, he knows we are a forgetful people. So what does he do? In his incalculable mercy, he accommodates himself to our needs. After all, that's why he came as a human being, so we could see him with our eyes, and touch him with our hands, and remember.[24]

God knows very well that we are frail and failing people with notoriously short memories. That's why down through the centuries and through the days and years of our lives, he gives us constant reminders. The apostle Peter, looking ahead to his own appointment with death on a cross, put it very clearly. Notice all the memory-related words in his swan song:

> I shall not fail to *remind* you of things like this although you *know* them and are *already established* in the truth. I consider it my *duty*, as *long as I live* in the temporary dwelling of this body, to *stimulate* you by these *reminders*. I know that I shall have to leave this body at very short notice, as our Lord Jesus Christ made clear to me. Consequently I shall *make the most* of every opportunity, so that *after I am gone* you will *remember* these things.[25]

Peter looked ahead to the future by looking back to review the past. Like a pedestrian about to cross a busy highway, he looked both ways down the timeline.

God knows that we need reminders—of what we said to God; of what God said to us; of what we decided as a family before God; of sins forgiven; of whispered promises in the night; of miracles and deliverances; of promises we have claimed; of God's call on our lives; of the sense of destiny he has burned into our hearts; of those many times when he met us, spoke to us, touched us, warned us, healed us.

These are the sorts of reminders that can

- restore our flagging hope;
- fortify our faltering faith;
- lift us from the clutches of depression and discouragement;
- protect us from destructive pride and foolish self-sufficiency;
- warn us away from hidden traps and snares of the evil one;
- turn us from destructive life directions;
- keep us from the futility of wasted potential; and
- help us to discern those tender, timely moments when we can pass along key principles to our kids and grandkids.

God has always been in the reminder business. He put a rainbow in the sky to remind us of his promise. He gave Cain a mark to remind people not to harm him. He gave Jacob a limp to remind him of their wrestling match. He gave Paul a thorn. He wove secrets of his character into the Tabernacle. He gave us his names as reminders of his character. He gave his people memorial days and feast days to remind them of his faithfulness. He instituted the Passover as a reminder of his deliverance from Egypt and the deliverance that is ours in Jesus Christ.

> WHAT WE NEED ARE REMINDERS THAT SPEAK TO US OF WHO WE REALLY ARE, WHAT GOD HAS DONE FOR US, AND WHAT OUR ULTIMATE DESTINIES WILL BE.

Jesus, the Son, gave us reminders as well: the bread and the wine;

the forever scars on his hands, feet, and side; the Holy Spirit to remind us of what he said.

Because we are such a weak, forgetful people, we tie ourselves to calendars, Day-Timers, and PDAs. We have watches that beep at us, computers that chime, and even little cards with microchips to record our spoken reminders. But these reminders only tell us where we're supposed to be or when we're supposed to show up. What we need are reminders that speak to us of who we really are, what God has done for us, and what our ultimate destinies will be.

That's why individuals and families need traditions, memorials, and remembrances. That's why we need to tell each other our stories. Not because they are *our* stories, but because we will find portions of each other in each of them. There is nothing new under the sun. For all their differences, our stories are amazingly similar. By telling our stories, we strengthen one another for the road of life ahead.

God, in his grace, will continue to provide us with reminders. In time and eternity, we are living out our stories and building memories. Remember them. Tell them—for your own sake, for the sake of your children and grandchildren, and for the sake of those beyond us on the timeline whom we will never meet until time itself is a relic of the past.

Your Journey on the Timeline

Impact Statement: Remembering is the springboard to action.

Summary

- Virtually everything of spiritual importance is dependent on memory. There can be no personal growth without it.
- "You must remember" is as close to a mantra as anything in biblical history.
- Memory loss is the most devastating spiritual toxin known to the human race.
- All of history and hope is dependent on God remembering.

- To God, remembering and acting accordingly are one and the same.
- Believers, by definition, are rememberers.
- Historical revisionism can kill you. You can't pass on, let alone live well yourself, what you can't remember.
- God's ancient words still govern our modern world.
- Remembering is the most important skill you can develop and the most effective exercise you can practice.
- We can't drive safely without a rearview mirror.
- We humans are forgetful beings. We need reminders.
- We need reminders that speak to us of who we really are, what God has done for us, and of what our ultimate destiny will be.

KEY QUESTIONS

1. Have you ever looked up the word *remember* in a concordance? How often does God use the word in the Bible?
2. Can you remember a half-dozen key Bible stories and their primary lessons? Could you "tell the story" if asked?
3. If you could choose only six key Bible stories to remember, which ones would you choose?
4. If remembering and acting are inseparable twins to God, could you say that forgetfulness and disobedience are at least first cousins? Why or why not?
5. When Satan managed to deceive Adam and Eve, how did he do it? Did he question history? Did memory loss play any role in the destruction of innocence and paradise?

MOVING FORWARD

Do a quick concordance study of the word *remember* and its derivatives. You'll be impressed.

4

MARKING TODAY'S
KEY MOMENTS

It has always fascinated me how God, who is completely unbound by time, relates to a time-bound people.

Why did he set a daily appointment with Adam and Eve, choosing to come calling when the shadows lengthened and twilight descended gently over Paradise?

He could have come any time. But every evening, in the cool of the day, when the sweet breezes carried the mingled, spicy fragrances from every corner of the Garden, "they heard the sound of GOD strolling in the garden in the evening breeze."[1]

God accommodates himself to time. He can live in it as well as beyond it. But because his great heart has always yearned for intimate fellowship with mankind, the masterpiece of his creation, he will walk through time with us.

He will also mark significant moments—both on the timeline of history and on our own small portions of it.

Just recently, as I was reading through Scripture, I came across a small, almost obscure example in an often overlooked book of the Old Testament. And it moved me.

It happened in a rather unusual season of Israel's national timeline, just prior to the Bible's four hundred silent years between the Old and New Testaments.

It was after the nation had been destroyed by Babylon and carried away into captivity. It was after a remnant had returned to the land, rebuilding the Temple in the heart of Jerusalem and restoring the city's walls.

For whatever reason, the people had become discouraged and cynical, allowing the freshness and excitement of renewed Temple worship to become routine. And *boring*. Even the priests serving in the Temple courts were only going through the motions, offering up blighted and diseased animals for sacrifice rather than giving their best.

The book of Malachi records God's indignation over the way his people had been treating him—indignation, and a broken heart.

"I have always loved you," says the LORD.
But you retort, "Really? How have you loved us?" . . .
"I am honored all over the world. And there are people who know how to worship me all over the world, who honor me by bringing their best to me. They're saying it everywhere: 'God is greater, this God-of-the-Angel-Armies.'
"All except you. Instead of honoring me, you profane me. You profane me when you say, 'Worship is not important, and what we bring to worship is of no account,' and when you say, 'I'm bored—this doesn't do anything for me.' You act so supe-

rior, sticking your noses in the air—act superior to me, God-of-the-Angel-Armies! And when you do offer something to me, it's a hand-me-down, or broken, or useless. Do you think I'm going to accept it? This is God speaking to you!"[2]

No, it doesn't sound like an era God would want to mark for all time. It seems more like a period of the nation's history he would rather forget. And yet he marks it anyway—for all time and eternity.

Why? What happened?

Nothing much. Nothing that would even make Section E of the *Jerusalem Post*. Probably nobody in the religious intelligentsia was even aware of it.

But the God of heaven was, and here's what the record says:

> Then those who feared the LORD spoke to one another, and the LORD gave attention and heard it, and a book of remembrance was written before Him for those who fear the LORD and who esteem His name.
>
> "They will be Mine," says the LORD of hosts, "on the day that I prepare My own possession, and I will spare them as a man spares his own son who serves him."[3]

A small group of God's people took the title seriously, and in the midst of their sneering, jaded countrymen, they found one another and joined hearts and hands. Together, they spoke well of the Lord. They bowed their knees and gave him the honor he deserves.

Was it a men's group meeting on Thursday mornings? A women's Bible study on someone's rooftop terrace? A seniors' weekly potluck? A band of twentysomethings who rejected the blasé pseudosophistication of their elders and grabbed hold of a live power line out of heaven?

The Bible doesn't say. But what the Bible does say is that God himself took note of their meetings and their hearts. And to whomever it was standing by the throne of the Almighty, God said, "Mark this now. Write it down. I want it in a book."

God, who created the timeline and owes no allegiance to it, made his own mark on it. The one who has never needed a reminder made sure he tacked one onto the wall of eternity.

And 2,400 years later, the heavenly Post-It is still there. In fact, we just read it. God is keeping a record of people's acts of righteousness, bravery, and kindness. He will not forget. And neither should we.

• • •

I remember the day we buried Art Bock.

Art was a grizzled old World War II veteran who regularly patrolled our church foyer. He had an indomitable spirit, and his standard response to the typical "How are ya?" greeting was always an emphatic "Fantastic!"

Was he really? I mean, actually *fantastic*? I knew very well that Art's life had been no picnic. Like all of us, he'd "won some and lost some." He probably had some regrets, along with the rest of us, and he'd certainly had his share of disappointments. But evidently he felt there was no sense in dwelling on them.

> "AN HEIRLOOM IS A DEVICE FOR INTER-WEAVING GENERATIONS, TOKENS OF TIMES REMEMBERED AND OF LIVES LINKED WITH OURS."
> — DAVID LOWENTHAL

After all, he'd survived combat in Europe as an infantryman. After that, even the worst of days was pretty much sunshine by comparison. His regiment had covered four hundred miles in fifty days in the spring of 1945. They had liberated thousands of civilians and taken seven thousand German soldiers captive. Art always felt as if he'd walked "most every square kilometer in Europe" that spring. No soldier ever fully recovers from that kind of rigor and trauma. Some are awarded the Purple Heart (and Art had two of them), but no soldier is left entirely unwounded. Still, Art always found the positive side of every day. And that left him feeling "fantastic!"

I began my portion of the timeline in the same year that Art was fighting his way across Europe. Born in the summer of 1945, I entered a world at peace, a world made safe and quiet by the hard soldiering of men like Art Bock and his fellow warriors. My world was a gift to me from Art and his buddies. So is yours.

When those men finished their fighting, I was too young to have known what they had experienced. But all through my childhood I felt I owed them something. Something deep. My own childhood was secure—even delightful. And though I never actually witnessed Art's sacrifice on my behalf, I saw the pictures, read the books, and listened with rapt attention to my dad's own stories.

Sometimes, when my dad and his friends gathered, I got to tag along. I admired how those men loved each other. Their stories became monuments in my soul.

We all owe our freedom to the millions of soldiers like Art, who paid the price in blood, sweat, and tears to vanquish the enemy, and who returned home to build in large part the country we live in today. A soldier never fully recovers from the ugliness of combat. It marks him for the rest of his life. And the older he grows, the deeper the memories penetrate his soul. But from 1945 to the present, Art and his fellow soldiers pretty much kept their suffering to themselves while all the rest of us enjoyed our freedoms.

WE CAN'T ALLOW OURSELVES TO FORGET. PERHAPS ONE OF THE MOST LOVING THINGS WE COULD EVER SAY TO A FELLOW HUMAN BEING IS, "I WILL NEVER FORGET YOU."

Ironically, the weekend before Art's memorial service, his old unit, the 304th Infantry regiment of the 76th "Onaway" Division, held its annual reunion. Art, of course, didn't make it to the reunion. Neither did the 216 members of his regiment who had given their lives in Europe.

Today, more than half a century later, I and every other person in that memorial service—and millions who never even knew Art existed—owe him and all his fellow soldiers a debt of gratitude. At the dawn of the twenty-first century, those WWII vets were dying at the rate of about a thousand every single day. We can't allow ourselves to forget. Perhaps one of the most loving things we could ever say to a fellow human being is, "I will never forget you."

"YOU HAVE NOT BEEN FORGOTTEN"

"Dying for freedom isn't the worst thing that could happen. Being forgotten is."

These words appeared in an ad with Tom Hanks's signature superimposed over a WWII helmet marked by a bullet hole, during the campaign to raise money for a national memorial in Washington, D.C. for veterans of World War II. They're nice words, with strong sentiment. But so what? What do we *do*? Do we just sigh, step back into the sunlight, and walk away like the war never happened? Of course not! We must never forget. If we do, another Hitler, Tojo, or Mussolini will render life on this planet miserable for future generations. George Santayana's dictum is very true: "Those who cannot remember the past are condemned to repeat it."[4]

As I walked out of Art's funeral, I vowed I would do everything I could to help my grandchildren never forget those old vets, whom they will never get to meet this side of glory.

Today, Art and his fellow soldiers have a memorial in our nation's capital. Art didn't live to see the World War II Memorial, which opened to the public in 2004, but I have been fortunate enough to visit it. I found it awesome. Overwhelming.

As with the nearby Vietnam Veterans Memorial, I was gratified to see people walking slowly, standing quietly, reflecting thoughtfully. Some, in deeply personal moments, laid offerings at the base of the granite columns. Particularly moving to me was an old, worn pair of soldier's spats. Who was the soldier who had laced them around his tired legs? Had Art worn a set of those? How many miles had those spats traveled? Which countries had they seen?

Old veterans and their descendants have graced the memorial with cherished gifts. I saw faded medals, worn photos, and lots of personal notes. One note in particular moved me. It was written to a young soldier who never returned from the war. His life had been cut short before he'd had the privilege of marrying and raising children of his own. But his extended family knew how to remember and how to teach the following generations. Attached to a WWII campaign medal, the note was written in a child's script and tucked into a corner where two slabs of granite met. Its very simplicity made it seem profound to me.

> Thank you, Uncle Morris.
> We wish we could have known you.
> You have not been forgotten.
> Your memory lives on
> with your brothers and sister
> and with your many nieces and nephews.
> God bless you.

Not long after I looked up from this note, an old gentleman in a ball cap with a WWII insignia on it passed near me. Linda, my wife, asked him about his military service. Humbly, he told us he had been an airborne trooper. He had jumped into southern France in the summer of 1944 as part of the liberation of Europe.

We thanked him for serving us and our family. That's when his emotions overcame him. With trembling lips and tear-filled eyes, this kind old gentleman, who'd been quiet about the war for decades, thanked us for the thought.

Something powerful happens when we make the effort to notice something significant on another person's timeline. Remembering matters. It is both honorable and Godlike.

I won't forget World War II and my dad's generation. Nor will I forget the Korean War veterans, or those who served with me in Vietnam. I will tell stories and try my best to draw my grandkids into them. With persistence and determination, there will be at least one family, the Weber clan, that will see their own personal timelines as part of a much longer, collective timeline. And because they know how to remember, they will be the kind of people who will build a future of security and significance.

> SOMETHING POWERFUL HAPPENS WHEN WE MAKE THE EFFORT TO NOTICE SOMETHING SIGNIFICANT ON ANOTHER PERSON'S TIMELINE.

As I walked out of the auditorium the day of Art Bock's memorial service, and again as I walked away from the World War II Memorial, I found myself with two seemingly conflicting urges. On the one hand, I didn't want to talk to anyone. All I wanted was some time by myself to reflect. At the same time, I had a desire to talk with *everyone,* to communicate the passion that filled my heart.

Reflecting and communicating. By God's grace, I will do both for the rest of my life. How about you? Will your family remember? Will you tell them stories? Will you build memorials to mark their hearts?

HOW TO MARK THE TIMELINE

How do you put a mark on the timeline—one that will prompt those who follow behind to stop and reflect on a certain truth? There are a thousand ways—some large and complex, others small and simple. One reminder may be a towering slab of granite. Another might be a tiny picture hidden in a locket. One of the best memorials is just a simple story, repeated often and passed on to the next generation.

I think the best reminders are the simplest ones. Personal stories, family lore, and little treasures and keepsakes passed from generation to generation. They're all memorials, marks on the timeline.

My dear friend Larry Libby understands the power of simple reminders. He keeps a very special "treasure box" of memorials. And those of us who know him well have come to treasure what he treasures. He writes,

> I keep a little stash of treasures in my bedroom. I store them
> (please keep this to yourself) in a small box covered with smooth,
> polished lambskin. It has my name on it in gold, and I hide it
> under the dresser. There aren't any diamonds in there or tiny silver
> keys to some lockbox in a Swiss bank, just a few things I've kept
> over the years because ... well, because I treasure them. There's a
> necklace of black beads, created and placed in my hand by a gypsy
> woman in some desolate corner of India. A plastic "stained glass"

elephant my daughter painted for me when she was five or six.
My grandmother's gold pocket watch. And a silver dollar.

I don't treasure the dollar because it's particularly old or
particularly rare or because it's worth $12.50 at some collector's
joint. I value it because of who held it and where it has been.
When I was in high school, one of my older brothers was a
young Marine heading for Vietnam as a medical corpsman. On
the day he shipped out, I handed him that silver dollar and said,
"I want you to bring this back to me." He looked at me and said,
"I will." And he did. A year later, after a lifetime in that place of
heat and sorrow and chaos and death, he walked back through
our front door in Eugene, Oregon. "Here's your dollar," he said.

Those are a few of the things I'll always keep. They may not
add up to much, but I treasure them.[5]

The memorials we build may be as small as a silver dollar hidden under
a dresser in a quiet home in the country. Or they may be as large as
several acres on The Mall in Washington, D.C.

They may be as unassuming as a pile of rocks beside a river. They
may be as fragile as a lock of hair.

They may be as thoughtful as a poem.

But whatever their size or form, they help us remember who we
are and upon whose shoulders we stand. And as we share them with our
friends and families we will tell their stories. We'll see to it that our little
memorials will rehearse the character of the past and plant the seeds of
the future.

As a Vietnam veteran, I was especially moved by one of the more meaningful memorials I've ever come across. As you may know, 58,253 men
died in Vietnam (or are still listed as missing in action) and are listed by
name on the Vietnam Veterans Memorial, also known as the Wall, in
Washington, D.C.[6] But four of those names appear on a most unique
living memorial.

One of my fellow Vietnam veterans here in Oregon, John Voracek, served as a U.S. Marine and is determined never to forget four of his fellow soldiers who gave their lives in combat beside him. John wears the names of his four friends tattooed on his back just below his left shoulder. John helped load the bodies of two of them into a helicopter for evacuation. And he's still carrying them on his shoulder. "I never want to forget these guys' names!" he says. John has made an unusual effort to stave off forgetfulness. For the rest of his life, every time he looks over his shoulder, he'll remember his buddies.

PILING RIVER ROCKS

Let's look at another memorial that marks the timeline to this very day. It's a story that has been told and retold for well over three thousand years, and it will continue to be told until the timeline merges into eternity.

As with many of the best memorials, this one is quite simple—nothing more elaborate than a pile of river rocks.

The story of this humble monument is recorded in the fourth chapter of the book of Joshua. You might say that Israel was still in its youth at that time. The nation had been born when the former slaves from Egypt passed through the waters of the Red Sea. They had received their birth certificate at Mount Sinai in the form of the Ten Commandments, and they had lived out their rebellious teenage years in the wilderness.

Now, poised on the very edge of the long-sought Promised Land, they looked forward to establishing their homes, building their worship center, and fulfilling their calling. But wouldn't you know it. Before they could take their first step into the land, they faced one final, and seemingly insurmountable obstacle—a fast-flowing river at flood stage. The normally languid Jordan River had swollen into a brown, churning juggernaut, possibly up to a mile across.

Israel, God's chosen bride, couldn't even cross the threshold of her new home unless God carried her. And of course he did. With a flourish! Instantly damming the surging waters somewhere upstream, God stopped the torrent, quieted the waters, and lifted his bride to the point that she didn't even soil her shoes in the flood plain.

It was a great moment, worthy of remembrance. And it must never be forgotten. God directed Joshua to erect a monument as a memory aid for the generations to come—twelve large rocks from the middle of the river piled up in a heap on the Canaan side of the river.

> GOD DIRECTED JOSHUA TO ERECT A MONUMENT AS A MEMORY AID FOR THE GENERATIONS TO COME—TWELVE LARGE ROCKS FROM THE MIDDLE OF THE RIVER PILED UP IN A HEAP ON THE CANAAN SIDE OF THE RIVER.

Sometime when you have a few minutes, read slowly through Joshua 4 and turn the memorial-building instructions over in your mind. Visualize the process. Everyone participated; each of the twelve tribes chose a representative. While the Ark of God held back the waters, the twelve chosen men stepped back into the amazingly dry riverbed. They walked to the deepest part of the channel, and each selected a stone so large it could only be carried on his shoulder. The stones were stacked carefully on the riverbank, thus establishing a careful memorial ritual, a reflective catechism.

Thoughtful questions were developed, and the story was shaped in a form to be repeated. Every child in each generation, when passing by the memorial would be moved to ask, "What do these stones mean?" And the parents would teach, the nation's heritage would be passed along, their national identity would be reproduced, and God would be glorified in each successive generation.

As I read Joshua 4, it strikes me how specific the directions were for how to build the memorial. God specified who was to be involved, how many stones were to be gathered—of what kind, and where to get them—and then how to place them.

They were only stones, common river rock. But now those simple stones were elevated to a place of high spiritual prominence because of what they memorialized.

It wasn't fancy, but it was richly deep with meaning. The memorial didn't require the efforts of a high-priced design team, who would stroke each other's artistic egos. The memorial was too important—and too personal—for that. It wasn't about *them* at all. The memorial was not intended to be admired for its human creativity; it was built, straight out of the riverbed, to remind the people of their faithful God, who would always carry them, his bride, across every threshold.

Down through the years of the timeline, men and women have sought to build impressive, ornate, vastly expensive memorials and monuments to honor the Lord. I don't presume to judge the motives of their hearts, and I'm confident our Lord takes note of every expression of devotion or labor of love from his sincere followers. (Just think of the craftsmanship and beauty he ordained for the building of his Temple.) Even so, it moves me to think how very humble and simple the monument of river rocks was. A pile of twelve smooth stones. No glitz, no glamour, no gaudy display of gold and jewels. But because God himself had designed the memorial, those dozen rocks were infinitely more precious than a ton of gold. And they were designed "to be a memorial to the people of Israel forever."[7]

WHAT COUNTS IN A MEMORIAL, WHAT REALLY STANDS OUT ON THE TIMELINE OF MY LIFE, HAS LITTLE TO DO WITH FLASH AND SPLENDOR, AND EVERYTHING TO DO WITH THE MOTIVES OF MY HEART.

Those humble rocks serve as a reminder to me that what counts in a memorial, what really stands out on the timeline of my life, has little to do with flash and splendor, and everything to do with the motives of my heart. In fact, the greatest monument ever constructed on the timeline was a simple cross of wood, planted on a barren hilltop. Even the angels are awestruck when they consider its meaning.

A GLIMPSE OF A NEW WORLD

Do you ever sense the Holy Spirit's voice, speaking in the quiet places of your heart, saying words like these: *Mark this time. . . . Never forget what I'm showing you right now.*

Sometimes we call them "aha" moments. They sneak up on us, and something we probably should have understood previously, but missed, suddenly breaks through our awareness and—*voila!* Things come together and make sense, stirring our imaginations. God gives us such unanticipated events as markers on our timelines, moments we return to in our memories time and again.

My friend Randy Alcorn had one such moment the first time he went snorkeling in Hawaii. It became a life-changing event for him. In later describing his experience, he wrote, "I saw countless fish of every shape, size, and color. And just when I thought I'd seen the most beautiful fish, along came another even more striking. Etched in my memory is a certain sound—the sound of a gasp going through my rubber snorkel as my eyes were opened to that breathtaking underwater world."[8]

NOT ALL THE EVENTS WE MARK ON THE TIMELINE WILL BE JOYFUL. SOMETIMES THE MILESTONES WILL REMIND US OF A GREAT LOSS.

Now, bear in mind that Randy has lived in Oregon all his life. He's seen the Pacific Ocean countless times—but never quite like this. His experience in Hawaii marked his timeline, and that milestone will be there for the rest of his life.

I remember him describing it when he returned, and the word *wonder* kept popping up. Soon thereafter, a new piece of artwork appeared on Randy's office wall commemorating the discovery. I didn't realize it at the time, but I think he was memorializing a life-shaping discovery that had stimulated his sacred imagination and intensified his curiosity about the worlds that lie outside our daily experience. Worlds like the undersea garden he discovered in Hawaii. And worlds like heaven.

In his definitive work on heaven, Randy writes, "I imagine that our first glimpse of Heaven will likewise cause us to gasp in amazement and delight. That first gasp will likely be followed by many more as we continually encounter new sights in that endlessly wonderful place."[9]

Not all the events we mark on the timeline, however, will be joyful. Sometimes the milestones will remind us of a great loss, the loss of a piece of our hearts—as with John Voracek and his shoulder tattoo. Even so, revisiting that mark, that memorial, can become part of God's healing work in our lives.

"WE WILL GIVE WHAT WE CAN. . . ."

Dana Gioia is a Californian of Sicilian descent with a great love for his heritage. Though I have never met him personally, I feel as if I know him because I lived with him, vicariously, through a great tragedy—the death of his young son. Through his poetry, I felt his heart and I met his brothers. His memorial to his son gripped my emotions.

When Mr. Gioia and his wife experienced the life-changing trauma of sudden infant death syndrome with the death of their son, they refused to forget the little life that had come to live with them, however briefly. Following a wonderful Sicilian tradition, they planted a tree for their son, and with it a small piece of the discarded umbilical cord.

And then, in his wonderful book of poetry titled *The Gods of Winter,* Dana Gioia gave us a rare and excellent poem, commemorating the event. Titled "Planting a Sequoia," the poem captures the subterranean emotions of life in such a way that the reader actually *experiences* the lines. That's how I met the poet and how he has influenced my life.

To be sure, at one simple level, the poem is merely about digging a hole and planting a tree. At another level, however, it calls us to examine our own lives, our own families, and our own pain. At still another level, perhaps most far-reaching, the poem invites us to consider our legacy.

The interplay of the living and dead is deeply moving. It inspires us to lay a course for those loved ones who will come behind us, and it motivates us to build our own memorials. Dana Gioia has not only blessed his own family through this memorial, but he has also blessed countless other families—including mine.

Planting a Sequoia

All afternoon my brothers and I have worked in the orchard,
Digging this hole, laying you into it, carefully packing the soil.

Rain blackened the horizon, but cold winds kept it over the Pacific,
And the sky above us stayed the dull gray
Of an old year coming to an end.
In Sicily a father plants a tree to celebrate his first son's birth—
An olive or a fig tree—a sign that the earth has one more life to bear.
I would have done the same, proudly laying new stock into my father's
*   orchard,*
A green sapling rising among the twisted apple boughs,
A promise of new fruit in other autumns.
But today we kneel in the cold planting you, our native giant,
Defying the practical custom of our fathers,
Wrapping in your roots a lock of hair, a piece of an infant's birth cord,
All that remains above earth of a first-born son,
A few stray atoms brought back to the elements.
We will give what we can—our labor and our soil,
Water drawn from the earth when the skies fail,
Nights scented with the ocean fog, days softened by the circuit of bees,
We plant you in the corner of the grove, bathed in western light,
A slender shoot against the sunset.
And when our family is no more, all of his unborn brothers dead,
Every niece and nephew scattered, the house torn down,
His mother's beauty ashes in the air,
I want you to stand among strangers, all young and ephemeral to you,
Silently keeping the secret of your birth.[10]

What do you think? Pure sentiment? Foolish emotion? An overreaction to death? Or is there something to it? When life smacks us in the chops, is it best to reflect and learn? Or should we just forget it and move on? You know the answer to that. Denial is never healthy. Reflecting, learning, remembering—these can improve the quality of our lives.

By refusing to forget, we learn to live beyond ourselves. We learn to live for those beside us and for those who will come along behind us. Your life is not about you. Live larger.

That pile of rocks beside the Jordan River reminded each succeeding generation that it had taken many, many people and many, many circumstances to bring them to that point. Some of their ancestors had been faithful. Some had not. But God was always faithful and always will be.

Our memorials—those marks on the timelines of our lives—remind us all that we have a responsibility for those coming after us. Contrary to the popular maxim of today's society, it isn't just *"me"* that matters!

Build a few monuments of your own. There are generations coming along behind you who very much need to know that you were faithful . . . and have their hearts pointed toward the Faithful One.

Your Journey on the Timeline

Impact Statement: Mark today's key events and draw power from them tomorrow.

Summary

- One of the most loving things we can ever say is, "I will never forget you."
- Dying isn't the worst thing that can happen; being forgotten is.
- God is keeping a record of people's acts of righteousness, kindness, and bravery. God will not forget. Neither should we.
- Memorials are simply memory aids.
- Memorials may be as simple as a pile of rocks, as small as a treasured coin, as fragile as a lock of hair, or as thoughtful as a poem.
- Memorials rehearse the character of the past and plant the seeds of the future.
- Remembering the past stimulates our present and gives hope to the future.
- The odds and ends of life can become power-packed reminders of the past and the people and values on which we stand.
- Memorials remind us that we stand on the shoulders of others and we have a responsibility to those coming behind us.

1. Have you ever told anyone, "I will never forget you"? How did he or she respond?
2. What have you done, specifically, to make good on that promise?
3. Could you show a trusted friend three or four "little treasures" that embody key memories for you? Do you have a collection, however small or humble, of keepsakes?
4. Do you keep your keepsakes to yourself? Or do you have a way to share them with others and in so doing share yourself and encourage others?
5. Do you make a conscious effort to memorialize the people and values that have shaped you?
6. Are you beginning to catch the vision for memorializing the things that matter?

MOVING FORWARD

Identify two or three specific memories that have affected you and/or your family. Begin now to create specific memorial items that will (1) solidify those memories, (2) embody their lessons, and (3) become concrete treasures to pass those valued memories on to those you love.

HONORING
REPEATED EVENTS

You would think, given our ever-so-brief journey on the timeline, that we would crave a kaleidoscope of changing scenes, colors, images, and experiences. You would think that life's greatest ideal would be opening our eyes to a new landscape every morning, experiencing a fresh set of circumstances every day, and a different climate every night. And further, you would think that such a merry carousel of flitting colors, tastes, textures, and aromas would empower and energize us for a stronger run on the timeline.

That's what you'd think.

And you would be wrong.

Picture this: It has been a long day at the office. I'm shot. The drive home is full of headlights and horns. I leave the car in the garage, hang the keys by the door, and head straight for my closet.

My *closet*?

Hanging in the closet is my favorite "leave it all behind" uniform. It's an old pair of sweatpants, kind of an obnoxious burgundy color, with the elastic gone from the left cuff. The university logo is long faded. Forget the "pause that refreshes," this is the *pair* that refreshes. When I put on these comfy old rags, the stress of the world goes away, the troubles drop from my shoulders, and I breathe more freely and deeply. Life comes into perspective. It may have been a rough day, but now there is a sense of fulfillment.

Why? Why these pants? Well, a whole bunch of reasons.

One, my son purchased them years ago while he was in grad school in England, and they bear the logo of his university. Two, his accomplishment of graduate school was the fulfillment of a dream for both of us. Years before, while he was still a kid in high school, he'd seen the movie *Chariots of Fire*. The true story of Eric Liddell so inspired my son that he sat up and said, "I'm going to go to school there someday." It became a turning point in his life. And in mine.

Flash forward a few years, and there's my son in England, living his dream. Flash forward a few more years, and now he's a mature man, using his education well, and with a family of his own. And here I sit in the living room, in the comfort of my grungy "memorial sweatpants," remembering the satisfaction of those dreams.

What are the old, familiar things that bring back the memories for you?

Maybe it's a certain rocking chair by a particular window. An old, chipped coffee mug. The sound of wind in the pines. The scent of lilacs in the summer twilight. A winding path through the woods that you could walk blindfolded. The hymn "Amazing Grace." An old Coleman lantern. The welcome bark of a well-loved dog. The musty, dusty, motor-oil smell of your old pickup truck. Psalm 23 in the old King James Version. An oak tree you climbed as a child.

The truth is, I draw more energy from the familiar than I do from constant change. I'm more ready for a day of new horizons, knowing that I have a ratty, old pair of sweatpants and a comfortable chair on the back porch to return to in the evening.

> "RETURN TO OLD WATER-ING HOLES FOR MORE THAN WATER—FRIENDS AND DREAMS ARE THERE TO MEET YOU."
> — AFRICAN PROVERB

Our little segments of the timeline are all too brief. But absorbing and managing the new challenges ahead of us may very well depend on those moments when we retrace our steps down the well-worn path and drink water from the old, familiar well.

• • •

One of my earliest memories as a young boy is of a ritual—a series of sounds, each distinct, signaling a movement at the start of a new day.

There was some creaking, some clanking, some tinkling, some rustling, and a little scratching noise. Now that I think about it, it actually went something like this: *creak–tinkle–clank–rustle–crunch–thunk–scratch–whoosh!*

The odd series of sounds, it seemed, greeted me virtually every morning of my early life. It was music to my young ears, and its most distinctive note was the gentle chime of iron against iron. Every time I heard it, I knew that everything was okay with the world. The message infused in this little morning symphony was one of security, provision, and warmth.

It was the sound of my father starting the fire.

The old wood-burning kitchen range was the functional center of our home. The morning ritual began with the floor creaking just a bit as Dad padded barefoot across the kitchen linoleum. When the creaks stopped, there was a quiet second. Then the little tinkle as Dad picked up the removable stove-plate handle. This was followed by the clank as he lifted the eight-inch circular iron plate and set it on the stove's iron surface. Then the rustle and crunch as yesterday's newspaper entered the firebox as tinder.

The thunk of wood on wood signaled the placement of the kindling. Then the match scratched across the stove's iron corner, and whoosh, the fire was lit. It was like clockwork. From the comfort of my nearby bedroom, I listened subconsciously for each little sound in the ritual. With each whoosh, a new day was born. Virtually every winter day of my early childhood began with the security of that familiar routine.

Call it a ritual, call it tradition, call it what you want, but the impact of those sounds was peace in my young soul.

TRADITION OR TRADITIONALISM?

Repetition is an excellent memory aid. Healthy traditions grow out of the regular repetition of meaningful moments, which build the best of memories. To this day, one of the great pleasures of my life—and one I truly anticipate—is when the family gathers around the warmth of a good fire. I think of those times when the Weber men have come together around the campfire at the end of a long day of hunting. At first, we all stare reflectively into the flames, eyes glazed, minds drifting. And then someone recalls a memory and recites it for the rest of us. Other voices join in, and throughout the telling, the story is enhanced, maybe even embellished a bit by other voices in the shadows of the dancing flames. In the process, minds are linked, hearts connected, younger souls shaped, character built, and the family heritage passed forward on the timeline.

It's the way we humans have swapped stories for millennia. It's the way we have remembered our history across the centuries. It's a uniquely human ritual, and one I suspect will never disappear.

Too often when we hear words like *tradition* or *ritual,* we may be tempted to think of outdated habits, whose meaning or purpose are long forgotten and perhaps best discarded. But we shouldn't think that way. On the contrary, traditions and rituals are intended to warm our hearts. If they seem formal and empty, it's only because we've made them that way.

It's important to note that there is a difference between *tradition* and *traditionalism*. Tradition is good; traditionalism is not. One is healthy, the other sick; one is nourishment, the other poison. Historian Jaroslav Pelikan states the difference concisely: "Tradition is the living faith of the dead, traditionalism is the dead faith of the living. And . . . it is tradition- alism that gives tradition such a bad name."[1]

The difference between the two words is essentially the difference between the dying mainline denominations and the growing evangelical churches. Traditionalism is dead and deadly; tradition, rightly cultivated, is nourishment for the soul.

> "TRADITION IS THE LIVING FAITH OF THE DEAD, TRADITIONALISM IS THE DEAD FAITH OF THE LIVING. . . . IT IS TRADITIONALISM THAT GIVES TRADITION SUCH A BAD NAME."
> — JAROSLAV PELIKAN

We are shaped and matured on our journey down the timeline. And the healthiest growth is often related to the richness of reflective tradition that con- nects us to the vitality of our roots.

Pelikan writes, "A 'leap of progress' is not a standing broad jump, which begins at the line of where we are now; it is a running broad jump through where we have been to where we go next. The growth of insight—in science, in the arts, in philosophy and theology—has not come through progressively sloughing off more and more of tradition, as if insight would be purest and deepest when it has finally freed itself of the dead past. It simply has not worked that way."[2]

No, life does not work that way. We learn best in the "processional process" of passing the baton. The sacred rituals and traditions that add meaning to our lives are well known. They are the ceremonies and cel- ebrations of any number of very special moments, such as weddings, births, baby dedications, graduations, funerals, and memorial services.

Some of the most far-reaching traditions are the simplest—like saying grace at meal times or the practice of devotional meditation in the morning.

Repetition is a central element of healthy tradition. Through their repetition, traditions provide perspective, a 360-degree view that helps us see the timeline past, strengthens us for the timeline present, and gives us perspective and direction for the timeline yet ahead.

THIS WAS YOUR LIFE

Having officiated at scores of funerals and memorial services during my thirty-five-plus years in the ministry, I've found one element in particular to be of great value to the surviving family members: telling the life story of the deceased family member. To my mind, this is one of the most important parts of the service. But when it is done by a "professional," with the limited information available from the sorts of obituaries or death notices typically printed in the newspaper, it seems to come up short. Those cursory notices may contain data and factual information, but it's hard to find the *person* in them.

I've learned to ask the family members to tell the person's life story the way they remember it. Oh, they don't have to do the speaking at the service—and quite frankly, there usually isn't time for long, rambling monologues, however well intended. What I usually ask people to do is write out their memories. I'm then able to compile the several perspectives and put together a warm and appreciative account of the person's life.

After the service, the family usually receives a printed copy of the story. Without fail they express great appreciation for the keepsake. Several have mentioned that their children who are too young to have known their relative well will one day be able to have a more personal and valuable understanding of the deceased family member.

Not every ritual is as momentous and formal as a funeral or a wedding. Rituals come in all shapes and sizes. Some are as simple and mundane as brushing our teeth. Yet have you noticed that when you skip over one of your rituals, something isn't quite right all day long? Funny, isn't it? But it's part of how God has wired us. Without rituals and traditions, our sense of significance and meaning is leached from our lives through the years, leaving our souls thin and pale. Without traditions, our lives tend to devolve into blandness or chaos.

One of my favorite traditions—and one shared by families across the nation—is Thanksgiving. America would not be the country it is without this holiday, both for its reminders of how our nation got its start when the Pilgrims left their homes in the Old Country to journey across the waves to a new continent, and for how it draws us all home. Though our society is increasingly transient, most of us still have a place we consider our *home*. And if we don't, we wish we did. The longing for home is foundational to our humanity, and Thanksgiving, centered as it is on home and family, is the quintessential American holiday.

> WITHOUT RITUALS AND TRADITIONS, OUR SENSE OF SIGNIFICANCE AND MEANING IS LEACHED FROM OUR LIVES THROUGH THE YEARS, LEAVING OUR SOULS THIN AND PALE.

Every year at Thanksgiving, millions of Americans experience a strong emotional pull toward home, and that weekend is usually the busiest time of the year for travel. Like some unseen gravitational field embedded deep beneath the surface of our lives, Thanksgiving centers our orbit on family, traditions, and memories. The inherent stresses and inconveniences of the trip and the preparations are soon forgotten, buried beneath the sentiment and joy of familiar rituals. For me, it isn't truly Thanksgiving without at least one piece of pumpkin pie. David Lowenthal captured the essence of Thanksgiving when he said, "Inheriting no more than a soup pot and a roasting pan, a woman finds her vital Thanksgiving legacy in recipes and an 'appetite for togetherness.'"[3]

STARTING A NEW FAMILY TRADITION

In recent years, my family has established a new summer tradition that gains momentum with each passing year. We've decided that every year as many of us Webers as possible will take the second week of August as vacation—and we'll all get together. In all, there are more than twenty-five of us, spanning four generations, including my octogenarian parents, my siblings and me, our children, and for the past several years now, our children's children.

The half-dozen or so great-grandchildren, with seemingly more born each year, are especially thrilled to be with all the cousins. This past year, the oldest family member was eighty-three and the youngest was just two weeks old.

Each summer, we gather at the same place—the homes of my brother and one of my sons, who live next door to each other outside the Central Oregon town of Sisters. Their two homes, on acreage in the piney woods, provide ample bedrooms and bathrooms for the entire clan, especially if a number of us guys sleep out on my brother's large front porch. The mild nights make sleeping outside inviting, and it serves to extend the conversations into the starlight.

The schedule is light. The agenda is zilch. The communion is rich. It provides a time and a place for long, relaxed conversations across the generations. Scattered as we are throughout the year by geography, time, and busyness, this special week has become something of a family time-out, and it reminds us of why we love each other. With all of our quirks and idiosyncrasies, we choose to lose ourselves in one another as a united family. We pass the corn on the cob and the benefit of the doubt.

The gathering is intentionally without pressure. People come and go as their schedules allow. It is inexpensive and completely free of the hubbub of the holidays. No decorations. No expectations. No Martha Stewart. We fire up the grill, eat off paper plates, and have a ball.

Not every moment is unscheduled, however. We eat breakfast and dinner together every day, and we have some other traditions we're in the process of establishing.

For example, Monday is our white-water-rafting day. The guided twelve-mile float on the scenic McKenzie River provides a sense of adventure, ample time for water fights among our multiple rafts, and a whole lot of smiles and laughter.

Tuesday is a day off for recovering, shopping, reading, and hanging out. There's usually a game of hoops somewhere along the way, a softball game in the evening if we feel like it, and of course, ongoing conversations among the generations. My mother repeatedly shakes her head, smiles large, and with noticeable emotion, speaks for all of us: "This is just heaven . . . just heaven!"

The gathering around the big table for meals is pure joy. The little ones struggle with the spaghetti and usually resort to using their fingers. The conversation is warm, the smiles are constant, the giggles frequent, and Mom says it again: "Oh, this is just heaven . . . just heaven!"

You're right, Mom—it is precisely that: an earthly foretaste of that heavenly family reunion around a great table yet to come.

No less an authority than God himself insists that his own family develop and sustain healthy rituals and traditions. He directed the families of Israel to gather several times each year to celebrate their godly heritage. The Feast of Unleavened Bread, for example, began on the evening of Passover and lasted for a full seven days.[4]

The Lord's Passover was never to be forgotten and always to be celebrated. He insisted on it: "Now this day will be a memorial to you, and you shall celebrate it as a feast to the LORD; throughout your generations you are to celebrate it as a permanent ordinance."[5]

As Tevye from *Fiddler on the Roof* might say, "Tradition is good for you." The apostle Paul put it another way: "Continue in what you have learned . . . because you know those from whom you learned it."[6]

Traditions sustain our values. And that's an axiom that turns my thoughts to one of the most tradition-rich parcels of real estate in our great nation.

THE LONG GRAY LINE

If you've ever stood on The Plain at the United States Military Academy in West Point, New York, you know what I'm talking about. They say ghosts walk there. Powerful, friendly ghosts. Hero spirits. They are the spiritual memories of bygone leaders.

The oldest military post in the nation, West Point brings the past, present, and future together in one seamless garment. The Academy understands that carefully kept memories are essential to the preservation of duty, honor, and country. An intentionally managed memory of rituals, traditions, and values is necessary, as the Academy's purpose statement insists, to provide the nation with leaders of character.

I've had the privilege of visiting the West Point campus a number of times. In different seasons, the climate changes, the temperature varies, and the wind shifts, but the memories don't change. They're like rocks. In fact, some of them are rocks—stately monuments to leaders and memorials to principles. And every day—winter, spring, summer, and fall—they broadcast their messages, lest today's cadets, tomorrow's leaders, should forget the timeline past from which the timeline future extends.

THE ACADEMY UNDER-
STANDS THAT CAREFULLY
KEPT MEMORIES ARE
ESSENTIAL TO THE
PRESERVATION OF DUTY,
HONOR, AND COUNTRY.

Today, more than two hundred years after its founding, the Academy retains its status as one of the nation's most revered educational institutions. How does an institution retain such status after two centuries? By never forgetting its roots, by deliberately remembering its original purpose, and by observing its established traditions. West Point has never strayed from its original vision to provide the nation with leaders of character. The intentional nurturing of memory, ritual, tradition, and values accounts for the Army's success in this regard.

In the first six weeks of cadet life, called "Beast Barracks," every plebe is issued a handbook, and the regimen of weekly memorization is laid out page by page. By the end of those six weeks, every plebe's handbook will have been wrapped and rewrapped in duct tape just to keep it together, and the content of every page will essentially be committed to memory. Among other "customs and courtesies" established during their training, the cadets are required, during week three, to memorize the monuments on the campus—their locations, history, and the heart of what they represent.

By the time the cadets have completed their four years at the Academy, all the memories will reside in their minds and in their hearts. From the oldest alum to the freshest candidate, there will be a sense of connection. Past, present, and future will be connected in the Long Gray Line.

Let me tell you about the experience of a young man from our church. Born and raised in Oregon, a state widely recognized for its central location on the Left Coast, and a state without a single active-duty military installation, this young man had no major exposure to the military. His father was of an age where military service had not been required, and there was no particular sense of national service in the extended family. There were no connections to the military in general, the Army in particular, or to the Academy whatsoever. That the family's pride and joy, in the form of their youngest son, would find his way into the Army at all, much less through the Academy, was an unlikely prospect.

But the young man was somehow intrigued. He applied to West Point and was accepted. Even then, with congressional nomination in hand, he still had no personal sense that this was something he would actually do. There was no connection, no legacy.

Then came a winter evening, a dinner, and a baptism into tradition. That night, the young man tasted it. Not so much the dinner on the table, but the spirit of the Academy. Invited to an event in Portland with a number of West Point alumni, he and his mother had driven through a typical Portland mob that was protesting U.S. involvement in Iraq. Such hostility was certainly not a setup for making any life-altering commitments, especially with Mom along. But that evening, in the presence of some old soldiers who had paid the price, a connection was made.

It was not a singular connection. There was no individual who stood out. It was larger than any single personality. There was a climate in the room. Not pushy, not loud, not macho, but something deeper and larger—almost palpable. The young man's mother described it to me as "an aura." You could see it in the eyes and hear it in the tones of the men's voices. It wasn't so much that particular words were spoken, but that a comprehensive message simply overshadowed the room.

Handshakes seemed to whisper, "Welcome. We hope you will join us. Ours is a freedom-loving and freedom-preserving fraternity. It's a fraternity that serves even the protestors outside the door. Please be at home here. You are our next and future hope. You will carry the baton, and we will cheer for you as you join the Long Gray Line."

My young friend had never laid eyes on the campus at West Point. But that night, his heart *felt* the institution, and he felt the sense of connection to something much larger than any single person or principle.

THE LONG GRAY LINE IS A BEAUTIFUL METAPHOR FOR THE SEAMLESS CONNECTIONS BETWEEN GENERATIONS OF WELL-TRAINED OFFICERS.

The Long Gray Line is a beautiful metaphor for the seamless connections between generations of well-trained officers. It is an apt description of the "eternal traditions and values" of the Academy's soldierly brotherhood and its nurtured sense of timelessness.

At the end of the day, however, it's only a military college. What happens behind closed doors in America's homes says a great deal more about our strength and future as a nation.

In a day such as ours, a day when marriages fail, families fracture, and virtually all of our nation's foundational principles are under attack, it is good for families to establish and hold to a few meaningful traditions—especially those that point toward the faithful and changeless God who loves us.

Your Journey on the Timeline

Impact Statement: Honor repeated events and build purpose into your future.

Summary

- There's a big difference between tradition and traditionalism. Tradition is healthy nutrition for the soul. Traditionalism is harmful poison. Know the difference.
- Healthy traditions are like handles. They help us get a grip on what is meaningful in life.
- Traditions bring the past, present, and future together in one seamless garment.
- Traditions ensure that none of us is left behind to exist as an island.
- Everyone, knowingly or unknowingly, leads a ritualized life.

- Rituals, rightly understood, are healthy habits that make sense of our lives.
- The regular sights and sounds of our lives become the little rituals that give us both order (routine, systems) and pause (meaning, reflection). The rituals of our lives help us to pay attention and to frame the moments and values that matter the most.

KEY QUESTIONS

1. Have you ever thought of yourself as a person who values ritual and tradition? Why or why not?
2. Can you list a half-dozen annual traditions that your family enjoys? Are they "thought-full" or pretty much "thought-less"? Can you specify two or three things you might do to make each of them more meaningful?
3. Other than eating, sleeping, showering, and brushing your teeth, can you name one or two meaningful rituals you observe every day?
4. Can you name one or two rituals or traditions you could add that would really enrich your life?
5. Do you have children or grandchildren? What traditions and rituals are you determined to practice with them?
6. Do you have three or four family stories that bear repeating from time to time when your clan gathers?

MOVING FORWARD

Think through a meaningful gathering your family has had in the past. Try to identify the elements that made it memorable for people. Begin to draw plans for incorporating those same elements into your next family gathering. Put it on the calendar far enough in advance to be most effective. In conversations between now and then, start to talk about the things you most anticipate. Don't be discouraged if everything doesn't come off without a hitch. It's a start. Build on it. Great traditions, by definition, take lots of time, repetition, and improvement.

THE IMPORTANCE
OF PLACE

Why do I find myself longing for a summer evening drive up the old Yakima River Canyon Road? Why do the reds and golds of the vine maples in the fall take me back a lifetime? Why do I love a cold and snowy winter? Why does the spirit of the mountains loom so large in my mind? Why do thoughts of places like the Teanaway River, Red Bridge, Peoh Point, and the Stuart Range stir my soul? Why is Cle Elum so much more than the name of a little coal mining town to me? Because it's my home. It's my place. Because this is the soil and climate where my roots grew deep—roots that are not easily pulled up.

Home. There is no other word quite like it. Home is the place where we feel as if we belong, and it belongs to us. Like no other place on earth, home is where we came to the world, and where the world came to us. It is at home that we know and are known. Throughout our lives, at the least expected moments, we find our minds flashing back to memories of home, and our minds will never let go of those places.

This identity with a particular place, this longing for home is completely universal, common to every human being. We've even coined a word to describe our longing for it—homesickness.

This connection to a particular place has come to us down through the ages. The Bible says that in the beginning "the LORD God planted a garden toward the east, in Eden; and there He placed the man whom He had formed."[1] God *placed* us, and we've been people of place ever since.

Abram, the father of our faith, after an ill-advised and nearly disastrous trip to Egypt, made the long journey across the Negev through Canaan "until he came to Bethel, to the place between Bethel and Ai where his tent had been earlier and where he had first built an altar. There Abram called on the name of the LORD."[2]

Jacob, heartsick and worried after leaving Shechem, gathered his family and set off for "Luz (that is, Bethel), which is in the land of Canaan, he and all the people who were with him. He built an altar there, and called the place El-bethel, because there God had revealed Himself to him when he fled from his brother."[3]

The apostle Peter, travel weary and facing imminent death, wrote a final letter to the important people in his life. In his mind's eye, one physical place on earth stood out in his mind in sharp relief. "We saw his majestic splendor with our own eyes when he received honor and glory from God the Father. The voice from the majestic glory of God said to him, 'This is my dearly loved Son, who brings me great joy.' We ourselves heard that voice from heaven when we were with him on the holy mountain."[4]

And what was the result of Peter's recollection of the Mount of Transfiguration? "Because of that experience, we have even greater confidence in the message proclaimed by the prophets. You must pay close attention to what they wrote, for their words are like a lamp shining in a dark place."[5]

Though his old body may not have been up to the journey, Peter went back in his memory to a place where he had seen the Lord with new and wide-open eyes and heard the voice of the Father roll across the sky like summer thunder. And what was that to Simon Peter? An old yellowed news clipping in a scrapbook? Not on your life. The message of that moment was as highly charged in those later years as it had been in his young manhood.

> "THE TIDE THAT CARRIES US FARTHER AND FARTHER AWAY FROM OUR BEGINNING IN TIME IS ALSO THE TIDE THAT TURNS AND CARRIES US BACK AGAIN. . . . THE OLDER WE GROW, THE MORE WE FIND OURSELVES RETURNING TO THE DAYS WHEN WE WERE YOUNG."
> — FREDERICK BUECHNER

Encounters with the living God on the timeline are something more than scenery that recedes in the rearview mirror. They are the substance of all that we are today.

• • •

A friend of mine who enjoys classical music told me he can hardly bear to listen to some of the beautiful pieces written by the nineteenth-century Czech composer Antonin Dvorak. As a fifty-one-year-old man, Dvorak came to America for four years to become the director of the National Conservatory. While in America, he wrote his most famous symphony, *From the New World*. But he also became deeply homesick for his beloved Bohemia, with its hills, rivers, pasturelands, and villages.

Listening to the composer's *Slavonic Dances* is like hearing the word *homesick* put to music. It's as if Dvorak turned his soul inside out to write this music, the longing is so deep and profound. My friend, when he listens, says he is pierced by homesickness for a place he has never been.

If you grew up in a series of homes and towns, you may not find your longing focused on a particular piece of real estate. For you, "home" may be a longing for the values, connections, and life-forming memories of childhood, or for some season of happiness in your life gone by— something, someone, or somewhere that claims a special corner of your heart.

Virtually everyone at one time or another finds themselves far from home, far from the familiar sounds, smells, scenes, and memories that shaped them. There are other places worth living in, but there is no place like home to strengthen the soul.

Frederick Buechner, writing reflectively in his later years, says, "We find ourselves remembering the one particular house that was our child-hood home. We remember the books we read there. We remember the people we loved there."[6]

We all have a longing for home. So we go there, if only in the sanc-tity of our own thoughts. Home anchors us. It is at home that we make the memories that shape our souls, our identities, and our futures.

EVEN KINGS LONG FOR HOME

No matter how far we may roam, how low we might fall, or how high we might reach, we'll never find a place quite like home. The sky is a brighter blue there, the air more clear and crisp. Even the water tastes better.

Tucked away in the recesses of Scripture is a tiny statement that has always fascinated me: "And David said *with longing*, 'Oh, that someone would give me a drink of the water from the well of Bethlehem, which is by the gate!'"[7]

I can understand the need for a drink of water. We all get thirsty, and most war veterans would tell you that you don't even know thirsty until you've been in battle or on a long military campaign. But why all the specifics? Why water from the well of Bethlehem? Why the well near the gate?

Isn't water just water? Evidently not. Must be there's no water like the water from home.

The story becomes even more intriguing when you put David's

request in context. David was dreaming of a drink of Bethlehem's water not long after he'd sung his last song.

"These are the last words of David . . . the son of Jesse . . . the man raised up on high, the anointed of the God of Jacob, and the sweet psalmist of Israel."[8]

By the time David had reached the sunset years of his life, he had done it all. As a boy, he'd fought a bear and a lion while protecting his father's sheep. As a youngster, introduced to the battlefield as a mere courier, he had killed a giant. All the people had been impressed with his prowess, especially the ladies, and the popular songs of the day reflected it. He'd enjoyed a soul-knitting friendship with a fellow soldier, Jonathan, that would be the envy of any man. As a musician, he had composed dozens of psalms. As king, he'd survived any number of threats to his throne. As a leader, he'd commanded the finest of soldiers. And he'd had to bury more than one of his own children.

David had been there and done all of it. And what did he want most?

A drink from home.

The dust of a hundred battles chafed in David's throat. But for all his battle-hardened toughness, the old warrior's heart drifted back to his childhood home, to the village well. No doubt David had played around the well as a young boy. Maybe it was home plate for his version of stickball. Surely he had drawn water there for his family. Was it the finish line for childhood footraces? And how often had he returned from a summer season in the hills with the sheep, his pace driven by the anticipation of a long, cool, thirst-quenching drink from the refreshing well of home?

From his early days as a shepherd in Bethlehem, David's life had grown from a cold, clean, rushing creek in the wilderness to a young stream with a strong current and deep pools to a wide, regal river rolling with stately majesty to the sea. And now, late in life,

> THE DUST OF A HUNDRED BATTLES CHAFED IN DAVID'S THROAT. BUT FOR ALL HIS BATTLE-HARDENED TOUGHNESS, THE OLD WARRIOR'S HEART DRIFTED BACK TO HIS CHILDHOOD HOME, TO THE VILLAGE WELL.

he wanted another taste of the headwaters . . . a pure, cold drink from his youth.

Once again at war, and once again living away from home, for the umpteenth time in his life, the king was tramping through the hills and ravines of Judah. Surrounded by his mighty men, he was encamped in a stronghold in the hill country near Adullam. Surely there was no shortage of water in the stronghold. An adequate water supply was, by definition, an essential part of any stronghold. That's what makes it strong. You can last there a long time with plenty of water.

Perhaps in the quiet of the night, stars familiar to the shepherd boy pricked his memory. Perhaps David's mind drifted back to his childhood when he slept the secure sleep of the child at home. Perhaps, lost in thought, he licked his dry lips. I can well imagine his heart retracing the familiar route over the rocky ridges and through the narrow valleys to the place of his innocence. To his home. To the sweet water of the well at the center of his childhood hometown.

WHERE TIME FALLS AWAY

I like to think David was experiencing the same fond feelings for Bethlehem that I feel for Cle Elum, what you probably feel for your hometown. A modern writer described the feeling like this: "Your hometown is like your language—you will never be as fluent in another place or another tongue. You will never own or owe another place as much. You will never feel as strong a tie to another state or, heaven knows, another country. Blood is thicker than water, and that is as true of motherlands as of mothers."[9]

ALL OF US FIND OURSELVES, AT ONE TIME OR ANOTHER, FAR FROM HOME, FAR FROM THE FAMILIAR SOUNDS AND SMELLS, FAR FROM THE SCENES AND THE MEMORIES THAT SHAPED US.

Like the seasoned old warrior in the sunset years of his life, virtually all of us find ourselves, at one time or another, far from home, far from the familiar sounds and smells, far from the scenes and the memories that shaped us. There may be some scars on our souls . . . perhaps a season of life we wish we could forget . . . and we're feeling stretched thin and weary.

There is other water available, of course. There are many other wells in many other places. But there is no place like home to strengthen the soul.

Lynn Anderson puts some of my own thoughts into words in the following account of returning to his boyhood home:

> We drove down through the gully, past the old well, and up toward the yard where my small-boy feet used to run. But I was not prepared for what hit me when we pulled up in front of the old house. Weeds and grass, waist high, had taken over. . . . The outbuildings had all crumbled into the past. But the old house still stood—alone—her features weathered by time and vacancy, yet her personality and character still intact. . . . Partly broken windows stared blankly. . . .
>
> For long moments I could only stand and stare back. Time seemed to fall away. I felt my bare feet running through the grass again. Heard my sisters laughing as young girls. Smelled Mom's cooking. . . . An ache several levels deeper than physical pressed around my heart. I reeled under the storm of nostalgia.[10]

A Ukrainian farmer named Ivan has felt "the storm of nostalgia" too. In his case, he travels home daily. Oh, he's not allowed to live there. Ever since that horrible nuclear accident at Chernobyl in 1986, the authorities won't let Ivan stay at home. They moved Ivan and his wife to Myski. But Ivan still goes home. Even during the long winters, he hooks his plow horse to the sleigh held together with baling wire and rides back to the homestead. He visits the family graves there. Sometimes he picks an atomic apple from the struggling trees.

Why? Why does the old man return so often to such a forsaken place? The answer is both simple and deeply profound. It's home. "I come here to *feel* my motherland," he says.

Some years ago, PBS did a televised feature called *Death of a Dream,* which looked at the decline of the family farm in the American heart-land. To the PBS producers, it may have seemed that the dream was dying, but to those living it, the dream was very much alive. Vernon Lund, a retired farmer in his seventies, treated the audience to a concert on his father's hundred-year-old harmonica. But it was the poem of a child that was perhaps most poignant. Written in a simple composition book, it expressed a powerful sentiment:

> *Then give me but my homestead.*
> *I'll ask no palace dome.*
> *For I can live a happy life*
> *With those I love at home.*

I have very similar memories of a hillside behind the house in South Cle Elum, Washington. That hillside was home to endless games of cowboys and Indians and hide-and-seek. Its slopes provided the momentum for major sledding in the winters' snows. And it was there, to my shock, that I killed my first bird.

In the midst of our gang's acting out the life of Davy Crockett, I chanced upon the bird while on the sneak. Thinking nothing of it, I hurled my handy willow spear at it. It never occurred to me I might actually hit it. But the heavy end of the willow stick thumped the hapless bird's head against a tree stump hard enough that it died right before my eyes. A one-in-a-million shot, and a lifelong memory. Killed my first wild game at age seven or so. Will I tell my grandchildren about it? Probably. When they're about seven. I'll tell them, because I remember how my own grandfather's stories intrigued and inspired me—to imagine, to reach out, to grow up.

HERITAGE GROUND

My grandfather greatly helped me to enjoy my childhood. Maybe that's because he never really had a childhood of his own. Orphaned at a very young age, he never much wanted to talk about when he was young. His childhood had been especially tough, and that may explain why he had little interest in his past.

But I did. After all, he was my grandpa. He'd made my childhood richer with the memories we'd made together. I loved him, and I carry his blood in my veins and his name as my own. So, on one occasion when I was speaking in Iowa, I took a couple of extra days and made a point of visiting the northeast corner of the state where Grandpa had served his time as a "slave."

I visited the old German Methodist Church nearby, and to my delight I discovered my grandpa's name in the register of baptisms just before the turn of the twentieth century. Was that where he'd found Christ as his Savior? Is that where my personal godly heritage had begun? My mind was filled with questions, and my heart was warmed with gratitude to God.

> I VISITED THE OLD GERMAN METHODIST CHURCH NEARBY, AND TO MY DELIGHT I DISCOVERED MY GRANDPA'S NAME IN THE REGISTER OF BAPTISMS JUST BEFORE THE TURN OF THE TWENTIETH CENTURY.

I was fortunate enough to link up there with a dear old woman in her eighties who was familiar with the local farms and knew which orphan had been assigned to which farm. She took me to the farm of the family whose name Grandpa had mentioned begrudgingly now and then.

I looked over the fields he had worked. I sweated in the hot summer sun that had browned his skin. I sat next to the creek where my grandpa had no doubt gone swimming as a boy to cool off after a long day of "slave labor." I watched the sun set to the west, the same direction where Grandpa eventually settled and raised his own family, and the *place* where I would come to know him two generations later.

Beside that stream, I thanked God for my grandfather. I took a few pictures to share with my children and grandchildren. I'm grateful that Grandpa fought his way through tough times, that he worked hard all his life, and that he loved his wife and kids—for a lifetime. I'm grateful that he fathered my father, and I'm grateful he gave me a leg up on my own childhood.

Yes, our life-shaping memories have much to do with "place." Maybe that's why, for so many of us, our childhood homes become monuments in our souls.

When my parents told me they were planning to sell the house I grew up in, I felt my stomach make contact with my throat. My roots are intertwined with the house's foundation, and trying to pull them up would be like attempting to replant the two-hundred-year-old oak tree that reigned over the house's front yard. I started to wonder what it was about a collection of wood, bricks, plaster, and glass that made it so hard to leave. After all, the things that give a house a personality—the furniture, kindergarten refrigerator sketches, and shoes by the front door—all go with you when you move.

Then it occurred to me: That house, with its crumbling stucco skin and water-stained bones, was the only one that had seen me throw a rock through my parents' bedroom window (as a kid), and has kept my secret all these years. It let us build a fire in its belly every Sunday morning. It watched me as I drove, tentatively, up its gravel tongue the day I got my driver's license.

A few days ago, I received a call from an old friend with whom I hadn't spoken in years. I was surprised how many fifteen- and twenty-year-old memories of our childhood meanderings she had retained in such shining detail. She recounted things as if they had just now happened to her. It was then I realized that no amount of repainting, resanding, or recarpeting could erase the time we'd spent under that roof. Just as we carry the memories of our beloved house with us, it will always keep the memories of us within it.[11]

The point is, when all is said and done, we are all people of place. We are all, to one degree or another, homegrown. Oh, I know it's fashionable and politically correct to think of ourselves as citizens of the world. After all, aren't we all part of the global economy, the global village? Yes, there is a sense in which none of us is an island, and the ripples of our lives extend far beyond our ability to see the connections. And yes, thanks to technology, the world is getting smaller. But let's not overdo it. We are people of place. In the final analysis, we're *locals*. We are *where* we are.

Bottom line, you cannot live where you are not. It is nonsense to think the real world is always somewhere else. Live *wherever* you are. Be there. Be yourself there. Create a home and stay. Early in our marriage, Linda and I began to develop something of a conviction: We wanted our children to grow up in one place, establish friends in one community, experience the same high school, and basically know where home was.

But the life of a pastor in this country seems to be a fairly mobile one. The average pastor moves every few years. So we prayed . . . and stayed. Some choice professional opportunities came and went. But we stayed. And our kids know where they grew up—one town, one home, one school district, and one church.

Have you noticed? The longer you stay in one place, the greater your sense of home will be. Katherine Dalton's words resonate with that truth:

> A kid who has grown up in ten different cities is not from Des Moines *and* Atlanta *and* Portland, Maine. He is from nowhere, and that is not healthy, anymore than it is healthy to be an orphan, or to lose your house in a fire. Losing your family or your home will not kill you, but it is a real hurdle, and the same goes for being without a hometown. . . . Those of us from a real place . . . with all the stories and strengths and oddities we can draw on to define ourselves, have it so much easier than those people who have the burden of needing to choose where they are "from."[12]

BORROWED HISTORY

Snow Anderson, of Santa Fe, New Mexico, feels the longing for place in her bones. She writes: "Like many immigrants to America, I longed for what I left behind. Now, finally, I'm planting my own roots. . . . I never quite adapted until I moved to New Mexico, a simple, rustic place not unlike my homeland."

While listening to a book on tape while driving, Anderson was drawn into what she was hearing and just "couldn't get enough" of it. She noted that the author was a Southerner who had lived all her life in one place. She was able to write about "eccentric relatives, quirky neighbors and places she has known since she was a child."

When Anderson told a friend how deeply she was attracted to the writer, her friend replied immediately and knowingly, "Borrowed history." To Anderson's surprise, she burst into tears when she heard those words.

Later she would say, "Borrowing history. It's what I've been doing since my parents immigrated to the United States in 1966, three weeks before my eleventh birthday. . . . Gone were my friends, the books . . . the uncle who taught me how to tell time, and my aunt who sewed clothes for me and my dolls. I would no longer spend summers in my grandmother's village, where day and night blended into one. . . . My colorful childhood had ceased to exist. . . . [I] yearned . . . for the aroma from the neighborhood bakery, the sound of my aunt's sewing machine, the grain bin and the oil lamp in my grandmother's old house. . . . Decades later, I still feel a sense of loss. . . . I search flea markets and antique stores for objects that other families might have passed down to each other."[13]

> "I'VE COME TO REALIZE THAT BY PLANTING MY ROOTS HERE SO FIRMLY, I AM NO LONGER BORROWING HISTORY. I AM LIVING IT AND EVEN CREATING IT."
> — SNOW ANDERSON

Snow Anderson has decided to make a go of it, putting down roots and living where she is. Determined to no longer just borrow history, she's going to make a little of her own. "It has not been an easy thing, this business of becoming American. . . . There are times, like when I walk my dog in the country outside Santa Fe, when the sights and sounds of horses, roosters, and donkeys so strongly evoke my childhood that I feel a deep sense of belonging here. I've come to realize that by planting my roots here so firmly, I am no longer borrowing history. I am living it and even creating it."[14]

Snow anticipates that those coming behind her will appreciate what she has passed along.

Let's close this chapter with the story of a man who, late in life, finds himself still anchored to a bit of land rich with memories of childhood and new life. It's not a hometown, but it's a special, almost holy, place.

JOZEF'S STORY

Jozef Glodek is ninety-four years old, and he just returned from a visit to the places of his childhood. Glodek cherishes a piece of land on the coast of Belgium, and on that small plot there is one spot in particular, beneath an old tree, that looks out over the water.

Every year at this time, he goes there. It is the spot where, nearly eighty years before, his father took his final step on a journey to make a better future for his son. The two, with only a compass to guide them, had walked nearly a thousand miles. The father had survived the Great War, lost his wife to a flu epidemic, and determined to give his son a better life in America, away from the incessant battlefields of Europe.

Sleeping in fields, under trees, and alongside roads, the two walked and walked. The boy learned that his father's father had been a baker who "couldn't make a loaf without a lecture, always talking about God, family, honor, and country."

Jozef's father, in ill health and greatly weakened by the strenuous weeks of walking, died within sight of the ocean that would take his son to America. It's a memory not to be forgotten, so Jozef, the old compass in hand, makes the pilgrimage to that place each year as a memorial to his roots.[15]

Sometimes, when you think about it, it gives you a touch of vertigo to realize we live on the surface of a spinning ball hurtling through darkness and mystery, or to remember that our relentless march along the timeline will never slow down until we step off the end of it. But the God of all comfort, in his kindness and mercy, gives us memories as we march. Within those sheltered places of our minds, he imprints the images of dear places and familiar faces that reassure and console us on our journeys.

It's all to remind us that home on this side of time is just a fleeting movie trailer of *The Home That Is to Be.* Life is all about walking toward that greater front door.

Because of Jesus, it's wide open.

YOUR JOURNEY ON THE TIMELINE

Impact Statement A sense of place and home means a stronger launch into the future.

SUMMARY

- We all have a longing for home. It is a human constant.
- Home is where you came to the world and where the world came to you.
- Every one of us is from somewhere.
- Our life-shaping memories often have much to do with our sense of "place."
- We cannot live where we are not.
- Life is one long journey that, regardless of time or distance, is always homeward bound.
- There is no place like home. All of our lives, we labor to be at home.
- Homesickness is a universal malady.

KEY QUESTIONS

1. If you were asked, "Where is home?" how would you answer? Why?
2. What do you think of as your hometown? Why?
3. What are your most vivid recollections of home—sights, sounds, sensations—as you remember and value it?
4. Have you ever been really homesick? What brought it on?
5. Do you know many people in their fifties? In their most transpar-

ent moments, have you noticed a theme to the things they
frequently chat about? What is it?

6. Are you closer to home now than you were ten years ago? How
so? What are the key factors for you? Values? Geography? Friendships? Family relationships? Keepsakes? Reunions? Nostalgia?
Maturity?

7. Why do you think the old adage "there's no place like home"
seems to persist in every culture and every era?

MOVING FORWARD

Plan a trip home, no matter how near or far it may be, even if no one
you knew or cared about still lives there. Write down the several sites
you intend to visit and your reasons for visiting them. Try to identify
their specific value to you. Do it in such a way that the lessons are com-
municable and valuable to people you know, and who know you, today.
Consider taking one or more of those people with you on your trip.

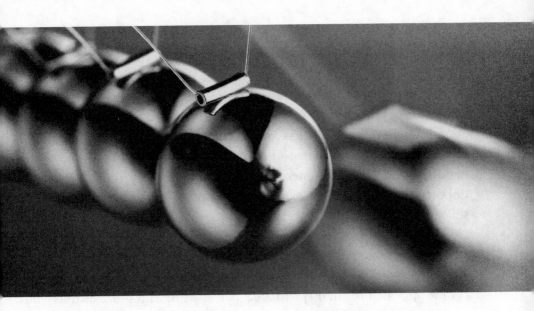

7

TRAIL MARKERS

When the battle was over and the ring of clashing swords and cries of the soldiers faded away, the Israelites looked across the hills and fields at the bodies of their enemies—and could scarcely believe what had just happened. God had given them a stunning, miraculous victory. Wide-eyed, they must have asked each other, "When we wake up tomorrow morning, will this even seem real to us?"

It would if the prophet Samuel had anything to say about it.

So he put a marker on the timeline.

The still-infant nation of Israel had gathered at a place called Miz-pah, where Samuel was to pray and intercede for them. It was a season of unusual spiritual openness for the nation. Scripture says that "all the people of Israel mourned and sought after the LORD."[1]

Samuel wasn't one to waste an opportunity like that. He sent out messengers with the command for all of Israel to gather in a solemn assembly where he would cry out to the Lord on their behalf.

If the prophet understood that this was a spiritual milestone in the nation, so did Satan, the enemy of God's people everywhere. He saw an opportunity to wipe Israel off the map once and for all. (These words still sound all too familiar today.)

While the people wept and prayed, the lords of the Philistines saw Israel's vulnerable position and quickly gathered their forces for a massive attack. As word of the enemy's rapid mobilization reached Mizpah, the people appealed to their spiritual leader in panic and great distress: "Do not stop crying out to the LORD our God for us, that he may rescue us from the hand of the Philistines."[2]

Samuel prayed, God heard, and he shook the earth with his answer!

"The LORD spoke with a mighty voice of thunder from heaven that day, and the Philistines were thrown into such confusion that the Israelites defeated them."[3]

The prophet knew his people well. He had no doubt that, left to themselves, they would quickly forget what had happened at Mizpah and return to their old pagan ways.

That's the way it is with the passing of time. God does something truly remarkable for us in direct answer to our prayers, and we thank him fervently. But then another day comes, the routine resumes, and the miracle is back behind us somewhere on the timeline. It so quickly fades from memory and no longer touches our lives.

That's why Samuel put a marker on the timeline.

"Then Samuel took a stone and set it up between Mizpah and Shen. He named it Ebenezer [Stone of Help], saying, 'Thus far has the LORD helped us.'"[4]

It was more than a stone with a funny name. It was a landmark in time. It was as if the prophet took a stake, drove it into the soil of history, and said, "To this very point, this very hour, this very moment, the eternal

God has stepped into time and space and intervened on our behalf. Never, never forget how the Lord has saved us and helped us in our great need."

Whenever we become aware of a situation where God, who is above and beyond time, steps *into* time on our behalf, we ought to place a marker on the timeline, even if it's only a deep scratch in our own memory.

> WHENEVER WE BECOME AWARE OF A SITUATION WHERE GOD STEPS INTO TIME ON OUR BEHALF, WE OUGHT TO PLACE A MARKER ON THE TIMELINE.

That's what God did when he took a piece of rough lumber and drove it into the bloodstained earth of a place called Golgotha. His own Son was nailed to that marker on the timeline. It was the greatest mark on history ever made. All of the timeline looked forward to that mark, and every moment of the timeline from then on looks back to it. Our modern calendar even hinges on that moment.

AD. *Anno Domini*. The year of our Lord.

To this day, many around the world carry a replica of that marker—fashioned in wood, steel, silver, or gold—around their necks and near their hearts.

Is the cross of Christ behind us on the timeline? Well, yes and no. It's behind us in the sense that it was an actual, literal, historical event. A true moment in time. But that same cross also marks the day when we bowed our knees to the lordship of Jesus in our lives and received his forgiveness and salvation. In that sense, the cross is with us every moment of every day and casts its healing shadow across the entire length of our personal timelines.

It's a good idea to mark our timelines in those key hours when we know that we know that we know God stepped into our lives and did that which only he could do.

In the eighteenth century, a twenty-eight-year-old man named Robert Robinson wanted to mark the timeline in a musical way. And he did, with a majestic hymn called "Come Thou Fount of Every Blessing." Within that hymn, the young Robinson penned these words, based on Samuel's memorial stone at Mizpah:

Here I raise my Ebenezer;
Here by Thy great help I've come,
And I hope by Thy good pleasure,
Safely to arrive at home.

Has God stepped into your life in recent days, giving you strength and grace, wisdom and provision beyond what you could have ever provided for yourself? Raise up your own "Stone of Help" on the timeline. And perhaps wandering, desperately unhappy men and women beyond your own lifetime will see that marker and take courage.

• • •

Some time ago, my wife and I, along with another couple, visited a holy place. Funny, I had never previously regarded it as a holy place. Taken by itself, it was very unimpressive. In fact, it was essentially only a hole in the ground. It was the site of my grandparents' homestead—or what was left of it.

My grandpa and grandma had long since passed away. Others had purchased and lived in the old house, at least briefly, since our family had moved away. And one of those people, perhaps more careless than my grandfather would have been, may have failed to keep watch over the old wood stove on a cold night. The result was that the home burned to the ground. And the only part of the home that remained, a home that had so enriched my childhood, was below ground—the cellar, the dirt basement.

> "GREAT EVENTS MAY TELL US LESS ABOUT THE PAST THAN THE TRIVIA ACCUMULATED BY ORDINARY PEOPLE— THE LETTERS, PRESSED FLOWERS, PROM PROGRAMS, CHERISHED TOYS AND THE LIKE SAVED BY THOSE WHO LOVED THEM AND COULD NOT BEAR TO THROW THEM AWAY."
> — WILLIAM MANCHESTER

In this primitive, old basement I had played hide-and-seek. So many memories were created in this place. There in the corner was the spot where my grandmother had warned me of the danger of the wringer on her ancient washing machine. She had said (with a reassuring smile, of course), "That thing could grab hold of you. You don't want to lose your arm, you know."

As we rummaged around among the remains, I stumbled across something of a treasure. Poking from under a charred board was a very old and blackened Mason jar of peach preserves. I recognized the sort. *It had to have been my grandmother's.* I recalled her carefully hoarding her supply of canning jars. "We'll need them again next summer when the fruit comes on."

Most of Grandma's life had been spent in the kitchen. I remember perspiration running down her forehead, and her gentle, gnarled hands using her apron to wipe her brow. As she caught me watching her work so hard, and saw my concern, she would pause, a smile crossing her lips and her eyes sparkling as she said, "Hard work is good for you!"

As I stood with Linda and our friends among the weeds and ashes, my mind began to wander . . . and wonder. Did my grandparents understand the impact their lives and faithfulness would have on so many others who would follow them on the timeline? Did my grandmother know how she was shaping her grandchildren? Could she even have imagined my writing this simple story about her, forty years after her passing? Could she have imagined my telling her great-great-granddaughter, my little five-year-old granddaughter, what Grandma was like?

Did she imagine how her grandchildren would live their lives? Do you? In our case, Grandma's great-great-grandchildren are growing up now around the same little Formica table she worked at in her kitchen. She's gone. The homestead is gone. But her influence lives on. Even though she's been gone for more than forty years, she still speaks. She may not be canning peaches anymore, but she's still shaping lives. And if you stand quietly among the trees surrounding the old homestead, you may still hear her voice on the wind. Her memory is still whispering stories. And that burned-out basement, that hole in the ground, has become something of a holy place to us, a monument in our lives.

I took my sons to that neglected plot of land when they were youngsters. And I'll take my grandkids there as well. And one day, we will all return there—to bury my aging parents, just up the hill from the old homestead, at the quaint little cemetery where many a coal miner lies at rest awaiting the Resurrection.

TREASURE, NOT TRIVIA

As we lingered on the holy ground of the old homestead where my childhood memories flooded over me, the couple with us began to reflect anew on their own heritage. Our friend Jan told us about one of her treasures. It was, as she described it, "a book my mom has taken the time to write to record a little of our family's history. But it's not the dates or places that make it most special. It's the people. And their stories. That's it."

> THAT BURNED-OUT BASE-MENT, THAT HOLE IN THE GROUND, HAS BECOME SOMETHING OF A HOLY PLACE TO US, A MONU-MENT IN OUR LIVES.

Someone once said, "Only two things will last forever: people and stories. And even the stories are about people." Jan's mom had remembered and recorded the stories of God's faithfulness to them.

She wrote of the year when she and her farmer husband had returned home from Bible school. There was no money, and they had seeds for only one crop—lettuce, of all things. So they planted what they had. When it came time to harvest, to their total surprise and joy, it proved to be the best market in many years for lettuce. Both the yield and the price were way beyond expectations.

We all chuckled as Jan finished the story. "Isn't that just like God?"

Things turned quiet for a moment, and then Jan said, "You know, by reading some of those accounts of God's faithfulness to our family in previous generations, our family today has been able to face our own significant difficulties, knowing he would be faithful to us."

She had said a mouthful. At that very time, Jan and her husband, Mark, were experiencing some of their toughest years together. Their business had fallen on hard times, and nothing seemed to be able to turn things around. Nights were long, and sleep fitful at best. The digits on the clock's face stared at them out of the darkness in the wee hours . . . 1:37 a.m . . . 3:26 a.m . . . 4:49 a.m. The pressure was enormous. But the reflective memories of generations gone by were beginning to refresh them.

There, beside a burned-out hole in the ground, a place so impregnated with memories, their lives began to come back into perspective, and strength began to seep back into their souls. Why? Because they remembered.

FINDING REMINDERS

It was late winter the day we visited the homestead, and the place had looked pretty bleak. The weather, cold and cloudy, seemed to reflect the season our friends had been going through. Just then my gaze wandered to a row of plants about fifty feet from the burned-out basement—my grandmother's lilac bushes!

We all had the same thought—*Let's dig up a few of those plants and take them home where the new generations are now blossoming.* Our spirits picked up, and even though the day was gray, we dug with palpable pleasure.

Our old station wagon must have looked a little peculiar rolling down the highway with a bunch of bushes flopping in the wind, their roots protected in garbage bags, but our hearts were lighter and we had a renewed perspective. In addition, we had a few reminders with us to plant in our yard—another connection to our past. It was a living milestone, transplanted from one part of the timeline to another.

> MY FAMILY AND I ARE LEARNING TO BUILD LITTLE MEMORIALS EVERYWHERE. WE HAVE WHAT SOME PEOPLE MIGHT CONSIDER "SILLY LITTLE THINGS" DISPLAYED AROUND OUR HOME.

My family and I are learning to build little memorials everywhere. We have what some people might consider "silly little things" displayed around our home. There's the dilapidated antique carbide miner's headlamp. My grandpa breathed a lot of coal dust wearing that lamp, all to feed my father, who fed me. I in turn fed my kids, who are now feeding their own. That old headlamp is a symbol of sacrifice and staying power.

There's an old, metal Pepsi case from the 1950s. It reminds me of the stories I heard while drinking a cold Pepsi with Grandpa. It was his favorite, and I never tip a can without thinking of him.

There's a smudged report card, with comments about yours truly, from my second grade teacher informing my parents that "he could be an exceptional student if he would only apply himself and talk a little less." My mom would have said I had ants in my pants. My kids got a kick out of that old report card, and any day now, when my oldest grand-child hits second grade, she will too. She's got the same ants in her pants!

On the fireplace mantle are my wife's grandmother's tiny reading glasses and her worn-out old Bible. They speak to us of our spiritual heritage. And there's the oil lamp we picked up on a trip to Israel in the 1970s. It dates to a thousand years before Christ and reminds us we're part of King David's spiritual heritage.

Mark and Jan's house is filled with treasures as well. "They don't necessarily fit the latest decorating trends," Jan admits, "and they would mean absolutely nothing to anyone else, but they speak volumes to those of us living and growing here."

There's a tired Stetson hat worn by a great-uncle, who, though he never had kids of his own, entertained countless kids in the community, bringing them to the farm to ride horses and enjoy a lost pleasure, the hayride. He gave himself away to others.

There's a scratched and dented canteen carried by Jan's grandfather when he went to France with General Pershing in the Great War. It reminds them of a man they know from family stories who was truly committed to the Lord. "We've never met him," they say, "but we will."

There's a front door, scratched and marred from a thousand passings in and out, brought from the homestead of great-grandparents who had immigrated from the Old Country. Now it occupies a special spot on a front porch still further west from its original setting.

"When they arrived in America," Mark said, "they had only each other, their Lord, and their dreams. Now we are those dreams." And there on the knickknack shelf are the small ceramic dolls of another grandmother who didn't end her life well. She'd made some poor and destructive choices. "But the dolls remind us we need to make more careful decisions—to stay on course, to finish strong."

Lilacs, mining headlamps, old hats, dented canteens, antique reading glasses, and old Bibles. For the most part, mere odds and ends of life, but they have become power-packed reminders of our past, our people, and the values on which we stand.

Looking back, past the beginning of our own timelines, you and I can gather strength, continuity of purpose, and a more meaningful context for our brief years under the sun.

HOW MUCH DO YOU KNOW?

How much do you know about where you came from? How much could you tell your kids if you were asked? Maybe you're the one to set it all down for the generations to come.

One of Jan's treasures is a simple plastic-covered, spiral-bound notebook written in 1997 by her dear Aunt Mary. It's maybe an inch and a half thick and is titled "Our Family Story: Graham-Lewis."

This book is a matchless treasure to the large, extended family. The introduction ends, "I hope you enjoy this story as much as I've enjoyed putting it into print." As a matter of fact, many of us who aren't even Aunt Mary's relatives have greatly enjoyed that book and its potent reminders of God's goodness to people living through the good and the bad.

> HOW MUCH DO YOU KNOW ABOUT WHERE YOU CAME FROM? HOW MUCH COULD YOU TELL YOUR KIDS IF YOU WERE ASKED?

Written engagingly in paragraph form, this family history avoids the usual abundance of charts, with a few photos interspersed. Chapters have titles like "Roy and Alta, How They Met and Courted." And then there's the chapter that intrigues me most called simply "The Letters." It's a collection of correspondence between Roy T. Graham and his bride-to-be, Alta Lewis.

The letters begin in October 1916, shortly after Roy and Alta met, and conclude three years later when Roy came marching home again from the Great War. Return addresses such as "Somewhere in France," and sign-offs like "Ever yours" and "So long, little girl" are poignant reminders of their strong ties to home during a time of such great sacrifice.

Roy was a man worth knowing. Imagine what would have been lost to his heirs if someone had not told his story. He survived the Great War, found his way home again, and married his sweetheart. Quiet and soft-spoken, he put on his bib overalls and straw hat and took up his hoe on the farm. Over the years he would build—with his own hands—two houses for the family. And the hand-powered mixer he used for the concrete now stands as a memorial outside the home where his great-grandchildren have grown up.

Way to go, family! Never let that mixer disappear!

Roy started every day early, milking cows, feeding sheep, and slopping hogs. He worked hard his whole life. But he was also a Baptist deacon, and his reading centered on the Bible and the *Farm Journal,* in that order.

> HOW WE ENGAGE THE PAST IDENTIFIES OUR PRESENT AND SHAPES OUR FUTURE. NURTURED MEMORIES FORM THE BASELINE OF OUR DESTINIES.

On Veterans Day every year, do you think Roy's descendants remember him with a sense of pride and belonging? You bet they do. Do you suppose they caught his work ethic? Yes, they have. Do they, too, serve Christ and his church with enthusiasm? Yes, they certainly do. Do they have a sense of responsibility to their country? I know they do. One of Mark and Jan's sons is now in the U.S. Army. I like to think that old canteen hanging on the wall may have played a small role in his choosing to serve in the military.

Memories are like that. How we engage the past identifies our present and shapes our future. Nurtured memories form the baseline of our destinies. I don't know who said it, but they were absolutely correct: "We cannot sail confidently into the future without the healthy winds of heritage blowing on our necks."

What a shame if we fail to connect with those who have gone before us on the timeline or fail to leave a legacy for those who will follow after us. What will you do to ensure those connections, those timeline links, among the generations?

Build some memorials around your place.

For the generations.

Your Journey on the Timeline

Impact Statement: Mark the trail to the future by leaving strong reminders of the past.

Summary

- The great events of history may tell us less about the past than we can learn from the simple trivia accumulated by ordinary people— personal letters, favorite pictures, cherished toys.
- The gentle winds of heritage blowing on our necks will carry us confidently into the future.
- Only two things will last forever: people and stories. And even the stories are about people.
- Personal treasures, rightly understood and remembered, can never become trivia.
- How we engage the past identifies our present and shapes our future.
- By reading of God's faithfulness to previous family generations, we are strengthened for our own difficulties.
- Decorate your home with simple little things from the past in order to connect the generations.

KEY QUESTIONS

1. Who are the people from your past who have influenced you the most profoundly? Why?
2. What experiences from your childhood can you recall that left an impression on you at the time? Was there a person? an event? an activity? a challenge?
3. Can you associate a symbol or artifact with those impressions?
4. Is there an item you remember most vividly from your roots? A picture? A clock? A book? A piece of furniture? Is it still in someone's possession in your family? Are you bold enough to explain its significance and ask to become its caretaker?

MOVING FORWARD

Pick one room in your home—maybe the den or the family room—and determine to decorate it in such a way that it gives identity to your family. Begin to identify small treasures you already have in your possession—pictures, books, letters, items of clothing, small artifacts that belonged to an older family member—and put them on display. Maybe start with just a single shadow box. Let the bug bite you gently at first. Enjoy its growth over time.

8

WHY ARE YOU HERE?

American novelist John Dos Passos, the illegitimate son of a prominent American attorney, was born in Chicago in 1896. Reared by his mother in Virginia, he lived for a time in France, returning to the United States to attend Harvard University.

In the middle of his education, World War I broke out, and Dos Passos left his college studies to join the Allied war effort—back in Europe again, serving as an ambulance driver in France and Italy.

Sometime in his long literary career, perhaps reflecting on those tumultuous war years, he wrote, "In times of change and danger when there is a quicksand of fear under men's reasoning, a sense of continuity with generations gone before can stretch like a lifeline across the scary present and get us past the idiot delusion of the exceptional. Now that blocks good thinking."[1]

I like that image: The long timeline behind us can become a lifeline.

• • •

Let's make it personal, in terms of your family history. If you're like me—an average person, from an average family, with nothing particularly noteworthy in your lineage, certainly no famous ancestors, no great wealth, and so on—you may not think you have a heritage worth the effort to discover. Maybe you've never really had much of an interest in these kinds of things. That was certainly true of me in my younger years.

Well, think again. Remember, our sovereign God makes no mistakes and participates in no accidents. So, you and your family history are no accident! You came from somewhere and someone, and it was all within the bounds of God's caring, sovereign hand. You are where you are on the timeline for a reason.

Think with me here. Think about God's absolute sovereignty as it relates to your family heritage, which for better or worse has come down to you through the generations.

The Bible tells us in very clear terms that God himself "gives all men life and breath and everything else. . . . He made every nation of men, that they should inhabit the whole earth; and he determined the times set for them and the exact places where they should live."[2]

Now that's a mouthful, and it's either true or it isn't.

As Christians, we choose to believe that the Bible means exactly what it says. And the Bible's teaching about God's

> WE'RE LIVING HERE AND NOW, IN THIS PLACE AND AT THIS TIME, BY GOD'S APPOINTMENT.

absolute sovereignty has some tremendous—and very personal—implications for us. So here's the point: You and I are not accidents. Not only that, but we're living here and now, in this place and at this time, by God's appointment.

There is enormous import in that realization. God's sovereignty tells us that God used our family roots to make us who we are to fulfill his purpose for us.

If God chose the time and place that we would live and if God knows when a sparrow falls and if God numbers the hairs on our heads (something of a challenge with some of us since it changes daily), then there are no accidents in our makeup. Our family roots are intricate parts of our design, whether we appreciate them or not. But we're wiser and more effective if we can see the hand of God in our ancestry and in our current circumstances.

YOU'RE NO ACCIDENT

You didn't come from just anywhere. If you believe your Bible, you also believe that in the divine sovereignty of the Creator of the universe, it was no accident that your mother married your father. Or that you were born to them. Or that their genes are your raw material. Further, it's no accident that your four grandparents were precisely who they were.

It was entirely possible, humanly speaking, that your great-grandpa might have married some other young woman. But he didn't. He married your great-grandma. And so it goes, on and on and on—for innumerable generations actually—all the way back on the timeline to Adam. The Bible explicitly indicates that it's Adam's spiritual genes that account for your being born a sinner. The point of your genes, your heritage, and your personal past in this book is pretty straightforward—you are no accident in God's economy. And your parentage—good, bad, or indifferent—is no accident either.

Your place on the timeline, short and fleeting as it may be, was determined by God himself. Your past on the timeline matters—as do the years before you entered it. And that's the point of the Bible's theology of remembrance—all the memorial stones, symbols, and passed-along stories that inhabit the pages of Scripture.

It's no coincidence that the generational theme of the "sins of the fathers" is treated very carefully in Deuteronomy, the book of the Bible most given to developing a theology of remembrance. The "sins of the fathers" is no small issue—and it carries a very real impact that is observable across the generations. Similarly, a father's solid character can have an equally potent impact from one generation to the next. The point is undeniable: You are who you are in no small measure because of the stock from which you came.

> YOUR PLACE ON THE TIMELINE, SHORT AND FLEETING AS IT MAY BE, WAS DETERMINED BY GOD HIMSELF.

Now let's get even more personal. The Bible says that God has "searched" you and "known" you. Intimately. He knows every speck of your person because he personally designed you. According to King David, God "scrutinizes" your path. He is "intimately acquainted with all [your] ways." He has "enclosed [you] behind and before. . . . [Your] frame was not hidden from [God], when [you were] made in secret. . . . [His] eyes have seen [your] unformed substance; and in [His] book were all written the days that were ordained for [you], when as yet there was not one of them."[3]

Yes, God has his hand on you all right. Now, in his loving presence, get to know who you are and then *live* like it, with a very personal sense of purpose and calling. Call that your heritage. Your roots.

THE HOLY SPIRIT LOVES GENEALOGIES

Ever wonder why God spends so much Holy Spirit–inspired ink on recording genealogies? why so much attention is paid to so many lists of long-lost persons? I mean, the folks in Scripture's lists have been gone for thousands of years. Why has God seemingly taken such an interest in recording those genealogies? I'm not sure of the full answer, but I can tell you this much for certain—it's because they're important to him. Those genealogies aren't space fillers in Scripture or throwaway pages. God takes an intense personal interest in them. And if it's important to God, maybe we'd better take it a bit more seriously ourselves.

Evidently, God wants you and me to be interested in these genealogies as well.

Do you every so often get a hankering to check out your roots? Maybe you've stumbled across an old manila folder full of scribbled notes and a family tree. Or perhaps an old photograph fired your curiosity. Then again, maybe your interest was piqued by a conversation with a very senior aunt at a family reunion, who had some information you'd never heard from your parents.

Or picture this: You're sitting around the fireplace with members of your extended family, browsing through an old photo album. Then to your surprise, your father leaves the room and returns with an old cardboard box. That's what happened to me. And it got me hooked.

I would never have anticipated what I experienced when my dad set that old box on the floor in front of us. I found myself overtaken by an eager, almost childlike, I-don't-care-if-it-is-past-midnight fascination with a stack of correspondence I found in there. Some of it dated back to 1902. There were other letters from the 1920s and 1930s, and still more from the 1960s. More than half a century of family history all in one box.

Those letters were every bit as absorbing to me as an intense detective novel. The difference was that all the characters in this drama were directly related to me—my ancestors, my blood kin. Those letters revealed part of the answer to how my life fits on the greater timeline. Their history is part of my history. In a sense, I'm standing on their shoulders. I owe them.

Once Dad hauled that box down from some dusty closet shelf, I was completely engaged with it. Busy as I usually am, I had to carve out time to look further into these things. Five minutes before, I hadn't even known such a box existed. And now I couldn't think of anything else.

DESPERATE TIMES IN THE BIG CITY

Imagine New York City, circa 1889, the dawn of what some have called the Gay Nineties.

Gay indeed. But not here. There was no gaiety in the face of the young mother who was walking, wandering, going nowhere among the filthy tenement slums, desperation written on every line of her face.

She had stepped off the ship from Switzerland five or six years before, and now in her early thirties she had three small children in tow—a boy and two girls—ages three, two, and newly born. But she had no husband. He had died the previous summer, like thousands of others in the city, from tuberculosis, which festered in the overcrowded slums. She was now beginning to feel sick herself. From that same killer disease? Very possibly. Whatever was she going to do? What would become of her little ones?

That desperate young mother, Lena Weber, was my great-grandmother. And the little three-year-old boy, destined to be orphaned before long, was my beloved grandpa, William Weber. He, along with his two sisters, Lena and Tina, was the subject of all that correspondence in the cardboard box.

Just a few years ago, I didn't even know who my great-grandfather was. As far as I knew and was concerned, my timeline past on the Weber side started and ended with my orphaned grandpa. There was no way of knowing who had come before him. For many years, all our family knew was that Grandpa's parents were German-speaking immigrants who must have arrived in America from Europe sometime in the early to mid-1880s. They likely had succumbed to the terrible conditions of the New York City slums, and they must have died an early death, because Grandpa and his sisters were orphaned very young.

FOR MANY YEARS, ALL OUR FAMILY KNEW WAS THAT GRANDPA'S PARENTS WERE GERMAN-SPEAKING IMMIGRANTS WHO MUST HAVE ARRIVED IN AMERICA FROM EUROPE SOMETIME IN THE EARLY TO MID-1880s.

Still, all these "must haves" were pretty much pure conjecture. All we knew for sure was that they spoke German and left three kids behind. We also knew that the three children ended up under the auspices of the Boys and Girls Aid Society of New York, riding what became known as an "orphan train" to Iowa in the mid-1890s.

But that scant bit of information effectively ended the "family tree" records, such as they were. Unfortunately, we Webers could trace our lineage no further back than a generation or two. Over the years, however, through conversations with a couple of cousins who had picked up some information here and there, we were brought up-to-date on a few disconnected bits and pieces. Still, it never quite fit together, at least to the point where I felt confident enough to tell the story. And I didn't have time to pursue it further on my own. Too much of my own life to live. Too many kids to raise. Too many soccer, football, basketball, and tennis events to attend. Too much ministry to pursue.

And what did it really matter anyway? I was as occupied as I could be living out my two inches of the timeline, and life was a boatload the way it was, without investing time chasing down family history.

Really, it's a shame that I had that attitude. And it was my loss.

ENTER THE BOX

That evening by the fireside, when the cardboard box entered my life, it gave me a bit of a jolt. It renewed my interest in the timeline rather unexpectedly. I had seen some of the pictures—or ones similar—before, but there were also documents I had never laid eyes on. And I was like a kid in a candy store. I couldn't pull myself away. We left my parents' house, and I brought the box home with me. In the wee hours of the morning I was still poring over those papers.

The modest stack included birth certificates, death certificates, and a few old military records. It also contained a couple of genealogical charts tracing some unknown ancestors back to 1641 in Switzerland. And then there were the letters. They kept calling to me. Why such intense interest? What could a stack of old letters possibly mean to me? They mattered because they were evidence of how God had actually marked out a time, a place, and a genealogical heritage for me. They reminded me of the passage from Acts I mentioned earlier:

From one man he made every nation of men, that they should inhabit the whole earth; and he determined the times set for them and the exact places where they should live. God did this so that men would seek him and perhaps reach out for him and find him, though he is not far from each one of us.[4]

I am who I am, I live where I live, I'm here when I'm here, during this precise stretch of history, and I will step off the timeline into eternity someday because a sovereign God has determined those things. And no matter what my present circumstances might be, God's strong desire is that I "would seek him and perhaps reach out for him and find him."

And, by the way, the same is true for you. God has us on the timeline exactly where he wants us to be. To do what? That's what we need to be constantly seeking! And it just may be that by understanding the two or three inches of the timeline that immediately preceded our own, we may gain some valuable insight.

We are not genealogical accidents! By God's intention, each one of us is utterly unique and called to a special purpose at a specific time in God's sovereign design. And the more we understand who we are and where we've come from, the more capably we can worship and serve God.

> THE MORE WE UNDERSTAND WHO WE ARE AND WHERE WE'VE COME FROM, THE MORE CAPABLY WE CAN WORSHIP AND SERVE GOD.

Who knows what you'll find when you start looking back? That's the hook with genealogy. And I know from firsthand experience now how people can become so gripped by it.

As far back as I've been able to trace, there are no "famous" ancestors involved in my timeline. Nobody who rode the *Mayflower* or fought in the American Revolution. No blue bloods. In fact, quite the contrary. We're talking orphans and paupers here. No-names. In fact, for a long time, there were literally *no names*.

But they're *my* orphans and paupers!

They're *my* no-names.

The attraction isn't a craving for notoriety or the hope of uncovering some fairy-tale romance buried in the past. It's simply the fact that these bygone orphans and paupers and others account for the very blood that runs in my veins. It's what their lives can tell me about who I am by God's divine intention that grips me. And when I see God's hand in my timeline, it prompts me to worship him.

I mentioned earlier that my orphaned grandfather, with whom I had a close relationship, never showed any real interest in learning more about his parents. He seemed to think it was kind of "humbug." They'd died before he'd really known them much. Life had moved on, and he'd made his way in the world, leaving the dark days in the past. His attitude was similar to that expressed by Rafiki, the mandrill shaman in *The Lion King:* "It doesn't matter; it's in the past."

But Grandpa's two sisters couldn't walk away like that. And clearly, his sisters' zeal more than made up for his apparent disinterest. Their search for their parents was decades long, desperate, and exhaustive. Letters often went unanswered. And it began with almost no information. Zero. Zilch. These three orphan kids didn't know much of anything about their past—not even their parents' names or their own birth dates. That's pretty basic information to have when you're trying to find your family. But when you are driven to know who you are, you can be very persistent.

A FAINT TRAIL

My two great-aunts, my grandpa's sisters, clung to a few scraps of incidental personal memory. One remembered holding a doll as she rode on the orphan train with her sister. The other had a vague childhood memory that *"my mother did not die until after we had been taken to the [orphans'] home, where a relative came and told us of her death."* Added to this was another foggy recollection: *"I had been taken to the home of some relative at first, but I was later taken to be with my brother and sister because I did not wish to be separated from them."* And there was an old Bible, whose inscription added a name, a place, and a date: *"Christina Weber, from Mrs. Algernon S. Sullivan, New York City, October 22, 1895."*

The women used every scrap of information they had.

The trail of correspondence wound through the Children's Aid Society to the Home for Seamen's Children to the Nursery and Child's Hospital of West New Brighton, Staten Island. It wound back through the Board of Health St. George, to Mormon church officials, and on to the Bureau of Vital Statistics of Manhattan Borough. It went by the Brooklyn Public Library, and it even included individual names and addresses selected quite desperately from the Brooklyn city directory.

THE CORRESPONDENCE
REFLECTS BOTH THEIR
DETERMINATION AND
THEIR DESPERATION.
A QUESTION IN ONE
OF THE LETTERS IS FULL
OF ANGST, "CAN YOU
PLEASE TELL ME WHO
I AM?"

The correspondence consistently reflects both their determination and their desperation. A question in one of the letters is full of angst, "Can you please tell me who I am?"

Another letter, something of a long shot, offered some pretty vague information. (But when that's all you've got, you use it.) The letter states, "I've always been under the impression that I was nearly school-age before I was separated from [my mother]. Any information or suggestions you can give us will be very much appreciated."

An additional piece of correspondence made reference to a tidbit of personal memory that might possibly be a door-opening clue: "My sister and I both recall clearly that we had a blind teacher of whom we were very fond. All the children called her Mary Lizzie." Teachers, be encouraged. The little orphan kids couldn't remember the name of the orphanage, but they could remember the teacher!

Sometimes a tiny scrap of recollection became the focus of broad inquiry: "It is my understanding that I was admitted to your institution sometime during the period from 1890 to 1895, and I am wondering if you could give me any information you may have on your records in this regard. Do your records show who my parents were? My parents' address? My father's occupation? Do you know who placed me in your care? Was it relatives? Or friends?"

Seemingly endless questions . . . but the sisters were making progress. Eventually, an official birth certificate was located. Now they knew for certain their parents' names. They were the children of Christian and Lena Weber. The search was picking up steam.

The trail got a bit warmer in a letter to a hospital administrator dated June 29, 1931: "I have recently learned that my mother, Mrs. Christian Weber (née Lena Birchmeier), was taken to your hospital during her last illness. She was admitted March 12, 1894, and I understand she died a short time later. . . . Any information at all will be very much appreciated."

The ongoing search for information and identity continued through official channels, but the "official" search was supported through every ancillary angle imaginable, including personal correspondence with anyone who might listen.

Years into the active search, a rich vein of information opened wide when one of my great-aunts received a letter that included the following paragraph:

> You mentioned once that you wondered if your folks had married in New York. We had all assumed that they came to this country together. But just on the one in a million chance they might have married in this country, I wrote and asked them to check the marriage records [in New York City, during a certain period] and was amazed that they found it. It took them so long that I gave up hope of ever hearing from them. Suddenly, it arrived. . . . So at least we know much more. I think perhaps they must have some new people in the records department as they certainly seem to be knocking themselves out to find anything I request.

Then came this blockbuster sentence: "They also found the death certificates."

Can you imagine? In the mid-twentieth century, when the three siblings were all well into their seventies, they finally located a copy of their parents' death certificates. And there was a surprise or two yet to come.

COMING TO AMERICA

Born in Obersiggenthal, Aargau, Switzerland, Lena Susette Birchmeier likely emigrated to this country, possibly with her sister, also single, in the early 1880s. In New York, Lena married John Christian Weber on October 27, 1884. My grandpa was born in January 1886, and his sisters were born in March 1887 and January 1889.

We know next to nothing of Christian Weber (as John was referred to on his death certificate), except that the certificate states he was a "leather worker." Born in Germany, he died at the age of thirty-two on June 30, 1888, after being in the United States less than six years. (I've since managed to find his name listed on a trans-Atlantic ship's manifest. My heart leapt a bit when I read his name on a document from 1882.)

Records indicate that my great-grandfather was buried on July 2, 1888, in St. Michael's Cemetery. Intriguing to me is the fact that I took my first breath fifty-seven years to the day after my great-grandfather died a suffocating death from tuberculosis. For the first several decades of my life, I had not once heard his name. In the years since, the search has turned up some interesting details.

John Christian Weber died in a House of Rest for Consumptives, meaning he died of tuberculosis, most likely contracted in the stale slum tenements on the Lower East Side of New York City. A little research told me that during those years the slums on the Lower East Side were the most densely populated piece of real estate on the earth, 986 people per acre—as many as 300,000 people per square mile. That's more crowded than today's Bombay, India.

When my great-grandpa died, Lena was left with nothing except the weighty responsibility of three little ones. The situation for her had to be overwhelming. Abandoned children, called "street arabs," were living all over the place. What could she do? How could she and her children survive in this hell?

Desperate, and likely homeless, Lena married Otto Frederick Feigenbutz on September 6, 1893. That summer, the nation had lived through the economic Panic of 1893, which had rendered New York

City's circumstances even more depressing than they had been—if that's even possible.

Six months after her marriage to Otto, Lena gave birth to another son, George, in March 1894. Evidently she had married to legitimize the baby. But Lena's weary body, overwhelmed by childbirth, began to give out. She was hospitalized. We don't know how, or by whom, but her son William and her daughter Lena were admitted to the orphanage—the Children's Aid Society—on March 12, 1894. Three days later, Christina, the youngest of the three Weber siblings, was admitted to the orphanage as well. Why the three-day gap? We don't know. Perhaps Lena, in her weakened state, had been desperate to keep her little girl with her just a little bit longer. But that's conjecture.

Lena Susette Weber, no address given, died at City Hospital, Welfare Island, on April 2, 1894, of chronic pulmonary tuberculosis. She was buried at Linden Hill Cemetery on April 4, 1894, in Grave 3, Row 11, Public Map 1E. According to her death certificate, she was thirty-five years old.

Her life was short and not sweet. But she was my great-grandmother, and that means something to me. What she did has affected my life. I like the fact that she was a fighter—a survivor, for as long as she could. I hope my life reflects some of her noble fortitude and determination. I'll hope to meet her one day in the real world to come.

My brother and I are talking about taking an extended trip to New York one day. Maybe we'll take up the "tag team" effort where our great-aunts left off. We've got our work cut out for us. But we'll do it. We've got a whole lot more information to go on than they had.

The history we will trace will not be a set of random happenings. No chance meetings, no quirks of fate, no coincidences. If you believe in the God of the Bible, there is no room for accidents of time and space. Right from the get-go, we assume that what we'll discover about the timeline behind us will have God's fingerprints all over it. And we also believe that what we learn on the timeline past will better equip us for the timeline future.

How about you? Any interest?

THE WAY WEST

I believe the Children's Aid Society of New York had the most noble of intentions in placing orphans on a westbound train. Considering the alternatives in that day, it was probably about as charitable a solution as they could devise.

I have since learned that the orphan train program helped thousands of orphans, and it probably saved my grandpa's life. Still, human beings being what they are, the tone of the phrase "supply of juvenile labor" may explain why my grandpa thought he had become nothing but a youthful slave in Iowa. It explains why the Iowa census of 1900 lists him, not with an *m* for "male," but with an *s* for "servant."

It may also explain why some of the correspondence from my grandpa's sister spoke of his being "beaten, overworked, and so generally misused that my brother ran away to battle his way" in the world at the age of fourteen. And it may also explain why my grandpa, a most truthful man by the time I knew him, lied about his age to join the U.S. Navy, just to escape it all.

I don't know about all that. But I do know this—in God's sovereignty, the Navy brought my grandfather to the West Coast as part of Teddy Roosevelt's Great White Fleet. And there he met the woman who would become my grandmother. Not by accident. Oh, I know it could *look* like an accident. They met on a battleship, the armored cruiser USS *Pennsylvania*. Gunner's Mate Third Class William Weber drew the short straw and had duty that Sunday afternoon. With the ship docked at the Bremerton, Washington, naval base, he was assigned to pass out ice cream cones to the public visiting the ship that day, while his mates took some shore leave.

Two of the visitors were a mother and daughter from Chicago who were taking a trip together to get over the death of their husband and father. When they approached the gun turret, William Joseph Weber handed an ice cream cone to Rose Dorothy Klotz, and the rest, as they say, is history. My history. And I have it on the authority of God's Word that *it's no accident* that William and Rose, now with the Lord nearly four decades, are my grandparents.

I also know this: My grandson, Stuart William Weber, is very proud to bear the name of his great-great-grandfather. He's not just part of the human herd, he's got roots. Roots that matter. I think it will make him walk a little taller.

The eternal God, outside of time, sees the entire timeline in one glance. He sees it as a continuity, and he also sees it frame by frame. I have come to learn that the continuity of my life preceded my birth, and it has an impact on the momentary "frame" in which I live.

> I HAVE COME TO LEARN THAT THE CONTINUITY OF MY LIFE PRECEDED MY BIRTH, AND IT HAS AN IMPACT ON THE MOMENTARY "FRAME" IN WHICH I LIVE.

No matter what you may think right now about your family history, the fact is you are standing on the shoulders of those who've gone before you. Would it encourage you to know who they were and how they made their way? Would it add some mettle to your soul to know that those who share your DNA made it through some pretty tough times? You bet it would.

If you don't know much about your ancestors, find out. Go back an inch or two—or maybe three—on the timeline. Don't quit. Discover who you are, where you came from, and—more importantly—*who* you came from.

Walk tall. And leave some broad shoulders for those still to come on the timeline ahead of you.

YOUR JOURNEY ON THE TIMELINE
Impact Statement: You are on the timeline for a reason.

SUMMARY

- Heritage is all we have to give to a world we will never see.
- *Things* matter only in the sense that they make connections and remembrances possible. Mostly, they help us tell stories.
- Put reminders out where you can see them so your eyes will remind your heart.
- Heirlooms are devices for interweaving the generations; they're treasures to be transmitted.
- Be a good steward of God's blessings in your life—past and present—by decorating purposefully around your heritage and opening your home.
- Photos, letters, quilts, pocket watches, teddy bears, old baseball mitts, memorabilia . . . it doesn't matter. The value is not in the things, but in the memories attached to the things and in the character and values transmitted to generations to come.

KEY QUESTIONS

1. Do a little open-ended brainstorming: Can you identify key memories that tell the story of your family? Think of . . . photographs . . . an old book . . . a particular smell that triggers a memory . . . an antique telephone . . . an old military uniform or medal . . . a cane or walking stick . . . a hunting rifle . . . a rumpled hat . . . a treasured set of dishes or silverware . . . an oft-sung lullaby . . . an old saddle . . . a favorite piece of antique jewelry . . . a 45 rpm record . . . a favorite holiday recipe. There's no limit to the potential stories and remembrances.
2. How can these stories be used to enhance your family's heritage?

MOVING FORWARD

Find another family member or a friend and begin to brainstorm over these kinds of heritage issues. Hint: The partner you're looking for is probably over forty-five years old. Or maybe it's not a family member but a good friend, the kind of person with whom you can be yourself. Begin together to build a mutual momentum toward intentionally preserving your heritage. You'll be surprised by how your enthusiasm and knowledge will grow.

I have to tell you one quick story: My wife and a neighbor a few houses down from us in Oregon began to talk about "this heritage stuff." One thing led to another as they chatted, and eventually they discovered an amazing connection. Though my wife and her friend were raised in very different parts of the country and had only met a few years ago, their mothers actually had the same maiden name. Wait—it gets better. It turns out their mothers' families, a couple of generations back, were both from the same county in Missouri. So my wife and her neighborhood friend are actually shirttail relatives. They've got the records to prove it. What a kick! You never know what you might find—and it's all part of your personal story.

9

THE CATAPULT

Because we have a God who views the whole timeline in a single glance, who sees the whole length of it like a bit of straw floating on a lake, it follows that he can do things within that timeline that defy human logic.

In opposition to every physical law, God can make a shadow on a stairway creep backward ten steps in order to reassure a godly king.[1] We've already considered "the long day of Joshua," where the Lord simply stopped the timeline for the sake of his warriors.[2] He can even take a man who has stepped off the timeline into eternity and place him back on the timeline four days later.[3]

When I received Jesus Christ as my Savior and Lord in a moment of time, what happened to the whole of my timeline? Did the effect of that eternal decision ripple backward on the timeline as well as forward? Smile if you like, but in my mind's eye I can see the Lord sending a bolt of energy back along on my timeline, at the instant of my salvation, touching the whole length behind me to the day of my conception.

The Lord told a timid young man named Jeremiah: "Before I formed you in the womb I knew you, before you were born I set you apart; I appointed you as a prophet to the nations."[4]

Did Jeremiah's decision as a boy or a young man to follow the Lord wholeheartedly ripple backward on his timeline and touch the moment of his conception?

Who can say? Scripture only gives us hints. For example, David writes, "You have hedged me behind and before, and laid Your hand upon me."[5] How do we respond to the revelation that God both walks behind us and ahead of us on the timeline? With David, we freely acknowledge that "such knowledge is too wonderful for me; it is high, I cannot attain it."[6]

As finite creatures, locked into the natural progression of the timeline, we view life in chronological order. We see David the shepherd boy and look down through the years at the young man who would become king and shepherd God's people, Israel. But God isn't locked into the timeline. In a sense, he starts with David as king and looks backward down the timeline to see what it will take to make a great king. And he touches the boy's life. He needs to fight lions and bears . . . and he will fight Goliath. He will run from Saul . . . he needs to know the wilderness and how to move about in it.

Have you ever walked with a Coleman lantern through a dark forest while you were camping or on a hunting trip? The same light that illumines the path before you also shines on the path behind you as you glance over your shoulder. The light goes both ways. Likewise, God's Word shows us both the way ahead and the way behind us by which we have come. If today we love God and seek his purpose and plan for our lives, Romans 8:28 assures us that all things will work together for our good. God tells us, as he told the tiny nation of Judah long ago, "I will restore or replace for you the years that the locust has eaten."[7]

All the days of my life have led me to this day, this hour, this moment.

God's Word is "a lamp to my feet and a light to my path."[8]

God redeems my path.

He touches my wasted years and squandered opportunities with grace.

Though my "sins are as scarlet, they will be as white as snow; though they are red like crimson, they will be like wool."[9]

Though I walk on a broken planet, soiling my feet in its mud, I am already a citizen of heaven, seated with God's mighty Son beyond the timeline. How can that be? Never mind. It simply is.

As the hymn writer Philip Bliss penned shortly before he took his last step on the timeline, "Hallelujah! What a Savior!"

• • •

I live in the upper northeast corner of Oregon's most renowned valley, in a town called Boring, Oregon—but never mind that. The Willamette Valley was a destination of legend in the middle to late 1800s when the wagon trains wound their torturous way across the virgin wilderness.

Those who survived the journey claimed their manifest destiny: a piece of river-rich soil—up to half a mile deep in some places—in a mild climate that to this day supports crops ranging from blueberries to wheat, corn to Christmas trees, hazelnuts to garlic. If you don't mind a little rain—well, maybe more than a little—this super-fertile valley lives up to its billing.

> "HE HAS HIS MOTHER'S EYES AND HIS GRANDFATHER'S SMILE. MAKE SURE HE HAS YOUR JUMP SHOT. MAYBE YOU DON'T HAVE THE NBA IN YOUR DNA. BUT YOU CAN PASS DOWN YOUR FADEAWAY . . ."
> — FROM A SPORT COURT AD

A red-ripe Oregon strawberry plucked from the vine on a dewy morning in late June may well rival the fruit once grown in Eden. No lie. And then there are the nurseries. There's probably no better place in the world for growing ornamental shade trees than the northern Willamette Valley. Chances are pretty good that if you live in the United States and have planted such a tree in recent years, it came from this verdant slice of Oregon.

My best friend for the past thirty-five years has made his living growing trees. In his more than three decades in the business, he's overseen the growth of—quite literally—millions of trees. If you ask him or any other tree grower, "What's the greatest contributor to a healthy tree?" he'll say, "It's the roots."

Ninety percent of everything that really matters to a tree goes on underground, out of sight. Roots are crucial to living things, and human beings are no exception.

We've all got at least some kind of fascination with our roots. How else can you explain an entire industry that has grown up around the subject of tracing ancestors back down the timeline? What drives so many people to this pursuit?

It's pretty simple, really. We want to know who we are and where we came from.

THE PAUPER AND THE PRINCE

William Lobkowicz has a story about roots. He was born in Boston in 1961, long after his family had fled Czechoslovakia to escape the chaos of World War II.

Forty years later (an entire generation) in 1989, while watching television, William realized he was seeing history unfold before his eyes. Europe was unraveling and—kudos to President Ronald Reagan—the Cold War had reached its frayed and ragged end. Spellbound with wonder, William watched live news broadcasts showing East German refugees jumping into the West German embassy in the Czech capital of Prague. Two new nations, the Czech Republic and Slovakia, were in the birthing process right before his eyes.

William's past called to him. "We made a decision to go back to

Czechoslovakia," he recalls. "We didn't know what was going to happen, but we wanted to be part of whatever the changes were."

What appears to be a rather innocent start to this adventure seems pretty quaint now—and almost too good to be true. The changes that have occurred since the Velvet Revolution in the Czech Republic have been monumental. And one of the biggest of those changes would affect the rest of William Lobkowicz's life.

In the 1990s the new Czech parliament passed several restitution laws touching on properties that had been confiscated by the Communists in the aftermath of World War II.

It turned out that William had some rather significant roots. It seems that the Lobkowicz name had quite a history, going back at least six centuries and connecting to multiple generations of the Czech upper crust.

Bottom-line, William discovered to his everlasting amazement that he was *royalty*. A blood prince. Even so, at this point he was only dimly aware of the implications of that discovery. He hired a lawyer to help him wade through the dusty pages of old regional records. Then there were two lawyers. Then more.

The researchers discovered that although many of the family's assets had eroded over the years, they were still vast enough that all the hard work had paid off. Big time! Something like nine castles' worth. The little beauty in which William and his family now reside has a hundred rooms. William opened several of the castles to the public as national museums, displaying six centuries of the family's valuable art treasures and innumerable other priceless artifacts. And all because he looked backward on the timeline.

> WILLIAM DISCOVERED TO HIS EVERLASTING AMAZEMENT THAT HE WAS *ROYALTY*. A BLOOD PRINCE.

Okay, chances are you're no prince or princess. Me neither. But I have learned a few things about my lineage—things that make me properly proud to be a Weber. There are no castles, priceless paintings, Beethoven manuscripts, stashes of rare coins, or books that predate Columbus. But I wouldn't trade places with William Lobkowicz for all the castles in Europe. My heritage has introduced me to treasures that are out of this world. My little orphaned, uneducated, coal miner of a grandpa, Lena's boy, was just a common man. He was not a high chancellor of Bohemia, but he was a servant of the High King of Heaven. And, in effect, he introduced our whole family to the King. We all look forward to the restoration one day of all that is ours as joint heirs with the King's only Son. Nine castles may look pretty insignificant on that day.

It's just a matter of time—and faithfulness. What we're really talking about here are *spiritual* genetics, a family line of faithfulness—a spiritual bloodline, so to speak. We are fully qualified as family by Christ's blood. It's all in his genealogy and in all sixty-six books of the Bible.

THE SCRIPTURES WE'RE TEMPTED TO SKIP

You've certainly encountered them if you've ever set out to read through the Bible in a year. You get your cup of coffee, sit in a comfortable nook by the kitchen table, and open your Bible, looking forward to a warm, devotional thought that will get your day off to a good start.

And what do you find?

"Mizraim was the father of the Ludites, Anamites, Lehabites, Naphtuhites, Pathrusites, Casluhites . . . and Caphtorites."[10]

Or maybe, "Their kinsmen of their fathers' households were Michael, Meshullam, Sheba, Jorai, Jacan, Zia and Eber, seven. These were the sons of Abihail, the son of Huri, the son of Jaroah, the son of Gilead, the son of Michael, the son of Jeshishai, the son of Jahdo, the son of Buz; Ahi the son of Abdiel, the son of Guni, was head of their fathers' households."[11]

The lists go on and on, and it's not exactly what you had in mind. Should you try to read them? Can you legitimately say you've "read the chapter" if you've jumped over the genealogies?

Why would the Holy Spirit invest so much inspired ink in those long lists of names that populate certain books of the Bible?

Evidently he thinks they're important.

Don't misunderstand. Our human ancestry is certainly not the be-all and end-all of our existence. As far as our standing with God is concerned, it doesn't matter if D. L. Moody, Billy Graham, and Mother Teresa are in our family trees. Ultimately, God has no grandchildren; we each come to him individually through the Savior.

Even so, he did create us in families. Our parents shape our lives, just as their parents shaped theirs—and so on, all the way back to Adam and Eve, the real first family.

Many books of Scripture contain significant genealogical information. This is especially true of the first book of both the Old and New Testaments. Genesis and Matthew connect many of the most important themes of Scripture through the use of genealogical lists. For example, Genesis 5 begins, "This is the written account of Adam's line" (NIV). And the next four chapters are built around a list of Adam's descendants.

Some of the great Genesis narratives are interspersed between lists of names. God has some specific points in mind for including those lists, and they play a key role in providing the context for (and therefore the meaning of) the well-known stories. Without the genealogies, we really can't grapple with stories such as the translation of Enoch, the corruption of mankind, the Flood, the rainbow covenant, the scattering of peoples, and the introduction of Abraham and his millennia-governing covenant.

In Matthew, the genealogies prove that Jesus was the only man alive in his day who had a legal right to the throne of Israel.

GENEALOGIES MATTER VERY MUCH—WHETHER YOU ENJOY READING THEM OR NOT. THE FACT IS, YOUR ETERNITY IS ON THE LINE.

Genealogies matter very much—whether you enjoy reading them or not. The fact is, your eternity is on the line. All of us trace our lineage back to Adam, and the Bible tells us that "in Adam all die." But because of the blood spilled by the Second Adam, Jesus Christ, we who have received him by faith have a new bloodline: "For as in Adam all die, so in Christ all will be made alive."[12]

In other words, what happened to Adam will kill you—the DNA of death lives in the genes of the whole human race—but those who claim the blood of the Second Adam will live forever.

Who you're connected to in your spiritual bloodline does make a difference, doesn't it? Your spiritual genealogy, in Christ, determines who you are and where you will spend eternity after you step off the bus at the end of the timeline.

FINDING OURSELVES

Seventy-seven-year-old Lorraine Lineer became something of a gene-alogist for a very simple but profound reason. "I wanted to find out, a little bit, who I am. In a large family, you see reflections of yourself in other family members, but I had no family to speak of; my parents were older when they had me, and I was an only child."

Can you hear the longing in Lorraine's statement? She was tired of being an "only." She was eager to draw her identity from something larger than herself. Good for her!

Every day, across the country, people are seeking to find themselves through a sense of connection with their roots. The largest genealogical records west of Salt Lake City are kept at San Francisco's Sutro Library, where hundreds of people pour through the doors seeking family information.

Clyde Janes, former reference librarian at the Sutro Library, notes that their discoveries are "virtually a religious experience. People come in and find information about their grandparent as a child and you see them reach out and touch the [computer] screen. . . . There's a spirit attendant to it, a spirit that moves people as they do it."

The well-known Christian writer Joni Eareckson Tada discovered some things about her lineage that allowed her to enjoy a certain sense of family pride and place:

> On a crisp morning in late winter, my sisters and I followed an intriguing branch of the Eareckson family tree. We left the western shore of Maryland, crossed the Chesapeake Bay Bridge, and made a right turn onto little Kent Island.
>
> Armed only with an old family map, we set out to locate the

original Eareckson homestead somewhere near Bat's Neck Creek at the bottom end of the island. We passed a few marshes, a stand of scrubby pines, and after asking at a few old farmhouses, we were directed down a lonely dirt road.

There it stood—a two-story, colonial brick home surrounded by woods and barren fields. We drove slowly around the ruts and potholes in the road and pulled to a stop at the side of the house. A couple of chickens pecked and scratched under the wooden front steps. A dog barked at us. . . . The place was empty.

We drove past the house out into the back field. According to our map, the family graveyard was nearby. Where the field crested slightly at the horizon, we spotted a large spreading oak tree surrounded by a plot of brush and tangled ivy. A likely spot.

Kathy, my sister, poked the base of the tree with a stick, pushing aside the ivy and twisted vines until she struck rock. There it was—a moss-covered stone with a crudely chiseled name: Benjamin Eareckson. And then another stone: Elizabeth Eareckson.

You'd have thought we'd discovered gold. We found a branch in the family tree and suddenly we were overflowing with family pride and an honest-to-goodness connection to colonial history. . . . I was bursting with pride and I didn't even know Elizabeth and Benjamin.[13]

Joni also discovered that the same lineage carried some pain. But that's true for everyone. You take the good with the bad. You sort through the bad, and you collect the good. You build on whatever positive side there is, and if you can't find anything positive, you can decide to become the pivotal generation. You can start the line that your descendants can be proud of.

In every human heart beats a longing to seek our roots, to find our homes, to put together a deeper sense of identity. It is our dream, and God has willed it so.

CREATING AN HEIRLOOM

A few years ago at Thanksgiving, four generations of Webers gathered around our family table. My brother and sister and I had decided earlier that we wished to make this an unforgettable Thanksgiving for the whole clan—something of a family memorial. We decided to create a family keepsake in the form of a written and photographic tribute to our aging dad and mom.

> WE DECIDED TO CREATE A FAMILY KEEPSAKE IN THE FORM OF A WRITTEN AND PHOTOGRAPHIC TRIBUTE TO OUR AGING DAD AND MOM.

We wanted their great-grandchildren, too young to remember a particular Thanksgiving Day meal, to be able to return again and again through the years to an understanding of their rich heritage. Have you considered a similar record of tribute for your family?

While Dad and Mom sat quietly, and a little uneasily, their three children, in the presence of the grandchildren and great-grandchildren, presented them with a special memento—a tribute of both pictures and words.

One of these days, we'll lay my parents to rest. As was true for every generation before them, the day will come when they will breathe their last. And it will fall to us who remain to bury them. What then? Will they be remembered? How will the generations to come identify with them? How will little Samuel Ryan Weber, their great-grandson now just a little tyke, ever come to know what they have done for him? Will he and his brothers, sisters, and cousins forget them?

I don't think so. There are a thousand ways to build memorials and monuments. There are a thousand ways to pass the torch. We'll tell their stories, and we'll pass along their cherished treasures. And by God's grace, we'll live their principles. Someday my parents' gravesite, on the hill above the little coal mining town where they met and started their family, will become a gathering place for future generations. We've already purchased the spot next to the graves of William and Rose Weber, from whom we take our name.

Yes, generations to come will visit my parents' gravesite next to the graves of their parents. And we'll reflect and remember. *Remembering* is good for the soul.

Gravesites are very much a part of our heritage, of remembering, of transferring the things that matter to the generations to come. Considering our own mortality is a healthy part of living well.

Sometime back, my parents and Linda and I visited the old coal miners cemetery above my hometown. We walked to the hawthorn tree that marks my grandparents' gravesite, and Mom and Dad stood next to us on the spot of their future graves. Nothing morbid; only a sense of God's sovereign grace and care. My parents have lived well, and their lives have made a difference. They see their aging as part of God's sovereign plan. So it was fun to watch them teasing each other about who gets which side.

Finally, Mom cracked us all up when she said, "Byron, honey, you take the side next to the road. You've always slept closest to the door."

Yes, we'll remember . . . and we will smile.

YOUR JOURNEY ON THE TIMELINE
Impact Statement: Find earlier marks on your timeline that will catapult you forward.

SUMMARY

- "[God] himself gives all men life and breath and everything else. . . . He made every nation of men, that they should inhabit the whole earth; and he *determined the times set for them and the exact places where they should live.*"[14]
- God is "intimately acquainted with all [your] ways. . . . [Your] frame was not hidden from [God], when [you were] made in secret. . . . [His] eyes have seen [your] unformed substance; and in [His] book were all written the days that were ordained for [you], when as yet there was not one of them."[15]

- God's sovereignty means you and I are not accidents of time, place, or genetics.
- Scripture suggests that God loves genealogy enough to invest significant amounts of Holy Spirit–inspired ink in the subject.
- Roots matter.
- We human beings, created in the image of God, have an inherent interest to know ourselves, to know *where* we come from, and to know *who* we come from.
- You are utterly unique, and you are not alone. You are standing on the shoulders of those who've gone before you.
- Get to know your family history. Take the good with the bad. Capitalize on the good; learn from the bad. And leave some broad shoulders for those coming behind you.

KEY QUESTIONS

1. Have you ever had an interest in your family's past? Why or why not? Be honest with yourself in your answer.
2. Do you think God actually has an interest in your personal development and how it has come to pass?
3. Can you see God's hand in your family heritage?
4. Could you articulate to your children, and your children's children, what value there is in their being a part of your particular family? Or are you content to let them think they're just part of the human herd trying to make their way in a cruel world?

MOVING FORWARD

Commit to at least the smallest of beginnings in learning something of your ancestry. Start with whatever scraps of information you have. If you don't have some kind of record already, begin to interview key family members to get started. Visit a Web site or two that may spur your interest. Browse some magazines on the topic. Try writing a bit of a narrative for your family. If you don't know where to begin, start with your own life story. Begin by getting started.

CARVING YOUR NAME
ON THE TIMELINE

People have strange ideas about chiseling their names onto the timeline.

Billionaire Donald Trump builds skyscrapers, naming one the Trump Tower.

Popular cultural icons such as John Wayne, Bob Hope, and Ronald Reagan have had airports named for them.

Former president Jimmy Carter had a younger brother who hungered for his own piece of immortality. Obviously not presidential material himself, this Georgia "good ol' boy" tried to leverage his brother's presidential clout to create a name for himself. So he launched a new brand of beer that bore his first name on every can.

Billy Beer.

Don't expect to find it on tap at the local bar and grill. The brand faded almost as soon as it was launched—and so did Billy Carter.

Others have had their names attached to stadiums, theaters, academic buildings, highways, bridges, and even diseases. In Oregon, the founder of Schnitzer Steel contributed generously to create a new performing arts center in downtown Portland, winning the privilege of naming the facility after his wife, Arlene. But I doubt either one of them was pleased by the nickname the theater acquired. Most Portlanders refer to it simply as The Schnitz.

If you have enough money, you can attach your name to almost anything. But if that's your one grasp for immortality, it will fall far short. The names may remain on a structure for many years, but they will be drained of all personhood. And most of the folks driving over the Smith Bridge will neither know nor care who "Smith" was. To them, it's just a construction of concrete and steel to get them from one place to another. And after they've driven over the bridge every day for a few months, it will virtually disappear from all conscious thought.

> "WHAT'S IN A NAME?
> THAT WHICH WE CALL
> A ROSE, BY ANY OTHER
> NAME WOULD SMELL
> AS SWEET."
> — WILLIAM SHAKESPEARE

How then, do you leave your name in such a way that people on the timeline ahead will remember *you* and value that memory?

I can give you an example of how one lady did it within the greater Weber timeline.

Her name was Rose.

• • •

No Weber has ever graduated from West Point, becoming a part of the Long Gray Line.

But we do have a Long Rose Line in our family.

And it's our prayer that our entire family will never lose the memory, character, and tradition of that Long Rose Line. It puts much of the fiber in our DNA.

The other day, I sat in a long, bare hospital corridor. The usual passersby (busy doctors, busier nurses, lost visitors, and so on) streamed by my fly-on-the-wall spot as I sat beside my brother-in-law. He and my sister were about to become grandparents.

During the wait of several hours, the attending physician, who is a member of our church and a family friend, stopped by several times. He was an exception to the busy current flowing past us. He leaned against the wall and chatted with us, keeping us up-to-date with the hard work my niece was doing in the birthing room nearby.

Suddenly the activity level picked up. The pace quickened, the bustle increased, and excitement rippled down the sterile corridor like a sudden gust of wind. And then, just like that, there she was! One minute we didn't know whether the new arrival would be a boy or a girl . . . and then we met *her*.

Kayla Rose Westerholm. The sound of her middle name—*Rose*—overwhelmed me. I didn't betray my emotions to the strangers along the corridor, but my heart actually moved, in a kind of stutter step. In an instant, my mind traveled several decades back on the timeline to my own childhood. Standing in that somewhat drab hospital corridor, my mind was filled with the brilliant colors of very vivid childhood memories.

Rose was the name of one of the most beautiful women in the world to me. It wasn't just a name; it was a vision, the very embodiment of femininity. As I stood admiring my lovely little great-niece, herself the picture of beauty, the memory of my grandmother overwhelmed me.

LEGACY OF A ROSE

I was not at the hospital the day Grandma Rose died. And over the years, the thought of her leaving this planet in the loving but helpless arms of her husband has saddened me. She was too good to die, too full of life to collapse on the way to get help, too dear to leave us like that. To me, she was larger than life.

Grandma Rose shaped me in ways that I am still, more than forty years after her death, only beginning to discover. She died when I was still a kid in public school, too young to understand how deeply she had affected my formative soul.

As a young student I always objected to Shakespeare's toying with my grandmother's name. Yes, I realize he predated Grandma, but I heard the line from her long before I heard it from him: "What's in a name? That which we call a rose, by any other name would smell as sweet."

I swear, the guy didn't get it. What's in a name? *What's in a name?* Only everything. That's all.

A name is neither just a word nor a label. It is a persona, an identity. Tamper with an identity and you do, indeed, change the fragrance. Change an identity, and you've changed the substance of the thing. At the very least, you confuse the message. *Things* don't have names; they have labels. *People* have names.

Okay, so we do name our pets, and my '52 Willys jeep has a name: Nelly Belle. That's because to me, she has a distinct personality. When I call her Nelly Belle, I'm not referring to a nondescript collection of nuts, bolts, and things that go whir. I'm relating to my faithful chariot, my doorway to another world. Nelly Belle takes me places I could not otherwise go. Yes, to some she's just a jeep. (Yes, she is a reflection of my childhood fascination with a certain early television program that featured a jeep of the same name.) But she's not just a jeep to me. In my personal world, she's taken on a persona of her own. Names matter. Names are one- or two-word descriptions for personal, relational realities.

THE PEOPLE OF ISRAEL UNDERSTOOD THAT NAMES ARE CRITICAL IN GOD'S FAMILY STRUCTURE. THEY OFTEN NAMED THEIR CHILDREN AFTER SIGNIFICANT EVENTS SURROUNDING THE BIRTH.

The people of Israel understood that names are critical in God's family structure. They often named their children after significant events surrounding the birth. Or they gave them names that embodied their hopes for the future.

When Rachel was dying in childbirth, she asked Jacob to name the son to be born Ben-oni, or "son of my sorrow." Jacob altered the request a bit and honored both his wife and his son by naming the boy Benjamin, or "son of my right hand." When the prophet Isaiah was born, his parents gave him a name that memorialized their hope for both their son and for the people of Israel, who lived under the oppression of the violent and brutal kings of Assyria. Isaiah means "Yahweh is salvation."

A PLAGUE OF TRIVIALITY

Names are meant to record great moments or to memorialize strong character. Names are also family monuments. Unfortunately, in today's society, many people do not appreciate the inherent significance of names. How else would you explain the spate of children named after the various brands that epitomize our empty materialism?

One observer captured our silliness in a single phrase, "Look, Nivea, it's your new little sister, Porsche." And then there is Lexus. Other popular names in the United States at the turn of the twenty-first century include Chanel, Timberland, and Armani. Some folks are naming their children after bottled water, alcoholic beverages, or hats: Evian, Fanta, Stetson, Chardonnay, and Guinness. Perfumes and cars seem to be very popular. How about a son named Pepsi? It's happened.

So what brand is your kid? Meet my son, the hiking boot. Or my daughter, the can of peas. Today's material culture has come a long way from the days of piety when people named their children Hope or Faith. The *Denver Post* ran an article describing one New York couple who offered the rights to name their child to the highest corporate bidder. Nothing apparently came of it, so they resorted to naming their little boy Zane, which they said was short for Zany.

Hey, if you have such an unusual name, don't fret. Just build into it a heritage that will elevate it above the trendiness of popular culture. Make it mean something to those who come behind you, something of solid character. If you're "a boy named Sue," be sure you're strong enough to make your detractors swallow their smiles!

I hope we'll choose to stick to a more meaningful catalog of names—names that memorialize the kind of character and aspirations we have for members of our family. Like the children of Israel, we must believe it is important to connect with the past in order to experience a meaningful future. We must realize the importance of being a part of something larger than ourselves.

I've always been struck by a single verse of Scripture tucked away in the story of the birth of the nation of Israel. It's the passage where Joseph tells his family, "God will surely take care of you, and you shall carry my bones up from here."[1] The day would come when Joseph's family would pack up and leave Egypt after four hundred years of living in that neighborhood. And they would take with them the family memories and treasures in such a way that the long line would remain connected.

> IT IS IMPORTANT TO CONNECT WITH THE PAST IN ORDER TO EXPERIENCE A MEANINGFUL FUTURE. WE MUST REALIZE THE IMPORTANCE OF BEING A PART OF SOMETHING LARGER THAN OURSELVES.

Their patriarch, Joseph, would die long before they would leave Egypt. The sons of Israel made a vow to carry the bones of their patriarch out of Egypt into the land of promise, the land of their ancestors. Such a commitment to memory pays off. Israel is an amazing family. They not only continue to exist today, after centuries of persecution and attempted annihilation, but they exist with an unbeatable spirit. They refuse to forget.

THE CHARACTER OF A ROSE

What's in a name? A lot that matters, regardless of what Shakespeare might say. The intentional memorializing of heritage and character is a vital trait of healthy families. Names and their stories are at the core of those memorials.

When Rose Klotz met William Weber on that battleship at the

dawn of the twentieth century, the die was cast for my life and the lives of my children, grandchildren, and great-grandchildren, though we would not enter the world until decades later—and, in fact, some have not yet even been born. On that fortuitous Sunday afternoon, when William handed Rose an ice cream cone and they exchanged names, it set in motion a legacy that continues to this day. Though it has been almost half a century now since Grandma Rose passed from this earth, she's more alive today than ever—in the presence of her Eternal King and in the character of her earthly progeny. Her character marks every generation of the Long Rose Line.

Here are some of that line's distinguishing marks, a few examples of what Grandma Rose's name represents to our family:

A Rose is servant hearted. Grandma taught us that it is a noble task to prepare meals for your family. She could make dirt a delicacy. Seldom seated herself, she fussed over everyone else until every need was met. From washing clothes to scrubbing floors to preparing meals to holding wounded hearts, she served others.

A Rose enjoys artistic appreciation. A fine musician, Grandma played the piano like very few in her era. Music was truly a fine art to her. In fact, her sister made her living as a professional musician. When, in advanced age, Grandma developed a tremor in her right hand, she retired from playing publicly, but the family insisted she continue to set the tone, tune, and rhythm in the home.

A Rose is sweet spirited. I never saw Grandma show the least bit of anger. Nor did I ever hear anyone recount a story of her being anything less than patient, kind, and gracious. Even when a rambunctious grandson, yours truly, thumped the floor so hard that a cake in the oven was destroyed, Grandma Rose merely smiled, chuckled, and said something in her native German that sounded like *krumenbrukly,* which I think means something like "busted up, time to start over."

A Rose shines with sparkle-eyed humor. She loved to tell me stories about her rascally brother and the creative pranks he played on others. She even got up on a chair one time to show me how to set a bucket of water on a partially opened door so as to douse an incoming victim without the bucket falling on the person's head. And when her hand began to tremble in her seventies, she didn't let it get her down. To the contrary, it became a fresh source of humor. I can recall her setting an empty drinking glass on the table before me, raising the pitcher of milk high in the air above it and betting me she could hit my glass with the stream of fresh milk in spite of what she called "the shakes."

A Rose personifies feminine grace. Grandma Rose was a lady. She never had much in the way of material things. After all, she'd married a kid who became a coal miner after he got out of the Navy. Really, she never had a thing. But she never complained. Grandma and Grandpa raised their kids through the Great Depression. Grandma ran their mini-farm, milked the cows, collected the eggs, made sauerkraut from scratch, scrubbed the kids, and handled what little money there was to manage.

When my grandpa married Grandma Rose, he was a young man who'd never been parented, didn't know how to scrub his own neck, and had never been held and loved. Grandma made a hero out of him. In some ways, I suspect she had to raise him right along with the four kids. But she did it in a way that totally protected his dignity, acknowledged him as the head of the home, tutored her daughter in the feminine arts, and showed her sons what it was to be married to a woman.

A Rose stands for godly prayerfulness. I saved the most important for last. All of my grandmother's characteristics flowed from her heart for the Lord. One of my most precious possessions is her old New Testament. Her precious handwriting graces the interior flyleaf. Like a personal name, one's handwriting is something of a fingerprint. I see her gentle script, and it reminds me of her gentle heart.

In the flyleaf of that little New Testament, she wrote the names of the godly women of the Bible. They were her models, and she studied them. Long before the word *feminist* was coined, Grandma studied what it meant to be a woman. Long before the militant feminist culture sprang up in the 1960s, Grandma Rose fostered a tender feminine heart. She demonstrated that a truly feminine heart is a godly and prayerful heart that expresses itself in grace to others. She gave herself away. She cared and she prayed.

Today, Grandma's New Testament is not gathering dust on a shelf. Far from it. It is the Bible that presides over all the weddings and funerals I am privileged to officiate. My prayer is that in life's most tender moments, Grandma Rose's character will rub off on the rest of us, including those who are married in the presence of her little New Testament.

Those who have come behind you, Grandma Rose, have found you more than faithful. What's in a name? A person. A memory. A character. A monument. A model from the past to anchor the future.

What kind of name are you leaving for your family? What kind of *line* are you anchoring? How are you passing the baton so that your family members are sure to catch it?

Here's a simple first step: Learn to appreciate the Roses in your life. Go out of your way to know your grandmother, grandfather, and aunts and uncles. You will be the richer for it, and so will they. And the line that flows from you will be healthier for it. Take a lesson from Sean McMeekin. When Sean's grandmother died in her bed in a nursing home in Rochester, New York, Sean wasn't there. Later he asked himself a hard question: "Grandma, where have you gone?"

> WHAT KIND OF NAME ARE YOU LEAVING FOR YOUR FAMILY? WHAT KIND OF *LINE* ARE YOU ANCHORING? HOW ARE YOU PASSING THE BATON SO THAT YOUR FAMILY MEMBERS ARE SURE TO CATCH IT?

> As is the usual case in my globetrotting life, I was thousands of miles away. . . . The news didn't exactly come as a surprise— my grandmother was over ninety years old; . . . still, though . . . I was appalled at the shallowness of my emotional reaction. . . . I couldn't even muster up a single tear for this wonderful old woman without whom I would never have come to exist. I never wondered about her inner life . . . what memories, what warm moments, what nuggets of wisdom would she have drawn on to ease her suffering? The sad truth is that I had no idea; . . . I never

really learned anything about who she was, what she really believed in, or what she had done with her life. . . . Unlike her, I was not raised in a Christian culture. . . . I was raised . . . to "express myself," to find my own way in the world, to esteem, above all, my own feelings, desires, and interests. . . . The explosive growth of the 'managed living' industry in the 1990s is eloquent testimony to a great generational disconnect. . . . It shames me to think of how little I have really done for my elders, or even to get to know them. But this holiday season, I am thinking of making amends. . . . It's really amazing how much . . . old folks have to say, when they finally find someone interested . . . enough to listen. . . . [I'm going to make a video portrait of my grandfather] while I still have a grandfather around. . . . I can't wait to learn more about what the guy was really like.[2]

Grandma Rose has been gone a long time now. Or is she really gone? No, not as long as she is remembered. And at many of our family gatherings for this birthday or that holiday, we find ourselves referring to Grandma Rose. Her passing is no longer calculated in years but in decades, but her Long Rose Line is very much alive, and by God's grace it will continue to march for generations to come.

Your Journey on the Timeline
Impact Statement: Carve your name on the timeline, and your name will endure.

Summary
- The act of naming is on page one of the Bible, a foundational mark of the image of God on human beings.
- Naming a child is a first step toward genuine interpersonal intimacy.
- Names are meant to personify character.
- Naming our children is a most potent form of remembering our heritage.

- Names both memorialize the past and express hope and expectation for the future.
- Things don't have names, only labels. People have names. Names are personal.
- Whatever your given name is, pleasing or otherwise, make it mean something honorable for those who come behind you.

KEY QUESTIONS

1. Have you ever worked through the meaning of your own name?
2. Did your parents have specific intentions in mind when naming you?
3. How have you approached the naming of your own children?
4. Whether or not your naming was intentional, what can you do now to give even greater meaning to your name?
5. Are you willing to alert others to the power in naming?
6. Are there names in your heritage that find themselves meaningfully repeated across the generations?

MOVING FORWARD

Take some leadership within your own sphere of influence with regard to the power of naming. Do it in your immediate family, your extended family, and your church. Prepare and deliver an appropriate lesson plan on the meaning of names in Scripture and the power of names in extending a heritage. Use your own family names when possible. Do what you can to influence your culture.

START RIGHT HERE

I've devoted the bulk of this book to the idea of building on the timeline behind you in order to maximize the timeline in front of you. Fair enough. If your family heritage is such that you can build on some solid positives, it's something I would strongly encourage you to do.

But even if the timeline behind you is pockmarked with negatives, you can still start right now, at this very moment, to build a better legacy for the generations that will follow yours. In God's incomprehensible grace and love, life can begin right now—with sins forgiven, failures put behind, strength given, and your future secured.

So you have no godly heritage, no worthy role models as far back as you can see on the timeline? No matter; God himself will give you a godly heritage.

King David, so lightly regarded by his family in his youth, later praised the Lord with these words: "You have heard my vows, O God; *you have given me the heritage of those who fear your name.*"[1]

Did you catch that?

If you come under the protection and authority of God, he will give you a mighty legacy stretching back to the beginning of time. *The heritage of those who fear his name.* That puts the bravest, most godly men and women in all of Bible history in your direct genealogy: Abraham, Joseph, Miriam, Deborah, Joshua, Samuel, Ruth, David, Josiah, Daniel, Anna, John the Baptist, Peter, Stephen, Paul. In addition to these titans of faith, you can look back in your family tree and see the clear-eyed, fearless martyrs of the first few centuries of the church, who refused to deny the name of the Lord in the face of humiliation, loss, flames, crosses, wild animals, and boiling oil.

In fact, they're all around you right now. Can you hear their voices from the grandstands, urging you on? The book of Hebrews speaks of "a great cloud of witnesses" urging us forward. One paraphrase of Hebrews 12 puts it like this: "Do you see what this means—all these pioneers who blazed the way, all these veterans cheering us on? It means we'd better get on with it. Strip down, start running—and never quit!"[2]

> HAVE YOU BEEN DISOWNED, DISREGARDED, OR DISRESPECTED BY YOUR MOTHER AND FATHER? DO YOU FEEL LIKE YOU'VE BEEN ROBBED OF YOUR HERITAGE BY THOSE WHO SHOULD HAVE LOVED AND TREASURED YOU BUT NEVER DID?

Some years after David penned Psalm 61, a later psalmist wrote, "*Your statutes are my heritage forever; they are the joy of my heart.*"[3] In other words, God has also given us the heritage of his Word. So, you can't seem to find any papers, any artifacts, any records or accounts of those who have gone before you? Your dad didn't keep a box full of letters, documents, and clues, as my father did? No matter; you have the mighty heritage of God's flawless, diamond-bright, razor-sharp Word, which will outlast the very planets and constellations he created.

Are you an orphan? Have you been disowned, disregarded, or dis-respected by your mother and father? Do you feel like you've been robbed of your heritage by those who should have loved and treasured you but never did? Be comforted; your heavenly Father has something glorious in mind for you. As David wrote, "though my father and mother forsake me, the LORD will receive me."[4]

Are you a woman who longed for the love and approval of a father, but never experienced it? Heed the words of the psalmist to the bride: "Your sons will take the place of your fathers; you will make them princes throughout the land. I will perpetuate your memory through all generations."[5] You are deeply, dearly loved and treasured by God, and he will never fail you nor forsake you. Not today. Not tomorrow. Not ever.

Do you long to return to a home and roots, but seem to have neither? In truth, you do have such a home. A place. You've never been there, but it's where you've always belonged. Jesus says, "There is more than enough room in my Father's home. If this were not so, would I have told you that I am going to prepare a place for you? When everything is ready, I will come and get you, so that you will always be with me where I am."[6]

The book of Hebrews describes a band of displaced, "homeless" believers, dispossessed by those who scorned any talk of Jesus and hated those who claimed his name. The writer calls them "strangers and exiles on the earth." Cut off from normal enjoyment of a home and family life, "they desire a better country, that is, a heavenly one." And the Lord who loves them has such a country, such a home waiting for them. Scripture says, "He has prepared a city for them."[7]

In our humanity, we may grieve over things that should have been ours but never were. We may mourn the loss of a precious sense of roots, family, role models, and heritage. But in Christ, God has seen to it that in a deeper, truer, more enduring sense, we don't lack anything.

• • •

I wasn't there, but I can picture the scene. It is February 17, 1869. A young couple wends their way through the unfamiliar streets of Hamburg, Germany. The wind off the North Sea is cold and biting, as it usually is this time of year. The small duffels they carry hold everything they have to call their own. It isn't much. But they do have each other . . . and their dreams. On the one hand, that is enough. They are thrilled to be deeply in love and to be departing on the adventure of a lifetime—traveling to America! On the other hand, they feel very much alone, lost, forsaken by their families.

"IF GOD IS FOR US, WHO CAN BE AGAINST US?"
— ROMANS 8:31, NIV

One of them is a German commoner, the other a high Prussian from a family of some status. It's reasonable to assume, because the young man is a meat cutter, that he is the one from the lower class. Forbidden to marry by their class-conscious European families, the couple have decided to elope and make their way to America.

Whatever heritage they may have had they are leaving behind.

They are starting over from scratch. Well, not exactly scratch. They do have a single treasure. They carry the map to that treasure in their duffel—directions to their new life in a new world.

Their map is a Bible.

Their treasure, one that no one can ever take away from them, no matter how alone or abandoned they feel, is a commitment to Jesus Christ.

Their precious Bible is tucked away among the clothing in their bags. They have determined that this holy book, and the people and stories in it, will be their guide. And if, by God's grace, they have children someday, that book will be the cornerstone of a new family in America. From February 1869 forward, *God would be their heritage.*

I wasn't there, but this scene on the Hamburg docks was a turning point on my personal timeline. The young couple were Heinrich (Henry) and Elizabeth Klotz—Grandma Rose's parents, and my great-grandparents.

They were entering a whole new world. Judging from the circumstances of their departure from Europe, and by the personal, handwritten covenant recorded on the cover of their Bible, they had resolved to leave their past and to become the pivotal generation in a new family. They were determined to establish a new line, a godly heritage. In Christ, they would discover the courage and the values that would enable them to build a healthy family that would thrive for generations.

One of my most valued treasures is a keepsake from this young couple, whom I never had the pleasure of meeting. It's the front cover of that cherished Bible, long ago torn from the old book of which it was once a part. On the inside of the cover, in typical nineteenth-century script, are the handwritten words, a covenant of commitment, from the two young lovers. Their words form the message they would leave to those who would come behind them. Their heartfelt note describes their departure from Hamburg and ends with these words: *"If God is for us, who can be against us?"*

A LEGACY BEYOND LEGACIES

"If God is for us, who can be against us?" Those words are taken from the apostle Paul's letter to the Romans. When Henry and Elizabeth set out for the New World, it seemed they had nothing but love, hope, and determination to carry them forward. But they actually had something even more important—an awareness that Christ and his Word would empower them.

Perhaps that is where you find yourself today—without much of a past to count on but with a strong desire to live well and pass on a legacy that matters. May I suggest that, by the grace of God, you already have everything you need to do the same thing they did and more.

Today, six generations of faithful Christians represent the legacy of that young couple who, in spite of their fears, determined to begin in a new way. You can do it too. I have it on good authority that Christ is the same today as he was in 1869.[8]

By the way, that single handwritten note on the cover of that Bible is the only existing artifact we have of my great-grandparents' lives. It's the only physical evidence we have—that, and the blood in our veins, the faith in our hearts, and the heritage we enjoy. Quite a legacy they gave the rest of us!

The young couple eventually made their way to Chicago, where they owned and operated a small retail butcher shop while living in the apartment above the street-level storefront. Over the years, God in his goodness gave them six children. My Grandma Rose was the next to youngest. That Long Rose Line may have been just a twinkle in the eyes of that young couple in February 1869, but that twinkle and their faithfulness affected their own generation and five generations of Webers (so far).

> THAT SINGLE HANDWRIT-
> TEN NOTE ON THE COVER
> OF THAT BIBLE IS THE
> ONLY EXISTING ARTIFACT
> WE HAVE OF MY GREAT-
> GRANDPARENTS' LIVES.

For all of us who have come behind them, their message on that simple Bible cover is a potent expression of both their love and their faith. I cherish it. And you know what? I plan to meet them one day, in the kingdom yet to come, the resurrected New Earth, where "there will be no more death or mourning or crying or pain."[9] That old Bible cover may appear to be just a leftover scrap to some people. But to me and my family, it is a great gift from people who blazed a trail for us—to America and to faith.

Why do I tell you that story? Because it's a story of hope for those who don't have much. I expect that many who will read this little book about heritage may feel a bit left out. So many in our world feel as if they have no heritage, no roots, no meaningful family background. Indeed, many people are alone in this world, and they sometimes feel like pieces of lifeless wood adrift on a rough and uncaring sea. For them, there is seemingly no heritage to receive and to pass down. They feel abandoned.

But, like the old hymn suggests, I've got news for you: "It is no secret what God can do. What He's done for others, He'll do for you."[10]

START A NEW TREND

Here's the point: If you have no godly heritage, I encourage you—no, I implore you—to *start* one. Commit yourself to become the pivotal generation. *You* be the one to start over.

No one has to be left out. No one has to be locked into a destructive generational pattern. Scripture is chock-full of examples of people who have grabbed the high-voltage wire of God's transforming power and changed their own lives and the lives of their families. Yes, heritage, or lack of it, is a potent reality, but it need not spell out your future. You can start a new trend. You may not have come from a healthy family of origin, but by God's grace and in his strength, you can start a new one.

You can launch your own heritage, from this generation forward—change the course of the river, change the trends, change your world. It can be done.

My great-grandparents did it.

So did Norm Norquist, whose story I told in my book *Tender Warrior:*

> SCRIPTURE IS CHOCK-FULL OF EXAMPLES OF PEOPLE WHO HAVE GRABBED THE HIGH-VOLTAGE WIRE OF GOD'S TRANSFORMING POWER AND CHANGED THEIR OWN LIVES AND THE LIVES OF THEIR FAMILIES.

Norm is a friend of mine [and an elder emeritus] at Good Shepherd Church—a spiritual patriarch. But his father wasn't. Norm's dad was angrily antagonistic when it came to spiritual things, and that created a lot of stress and pain in the home. But Norm determined he would do it differently. He would do it right. He would father a new and healthy family. He would be spiritually oriented. Norm and Dottie had six boys. (Then they "gave up" and adopted two girls.) Today those children have married and had children of their own—lots of children! Because some of them followed their parents' examples and adopted children in addition to their biological children, Norm and Dottie enjoy [more than thirty] grandchildren, and are still counting. That vibrant Norquist family is at the heart of our church.

Grandparents, parents, grandchildren, and now great-grandchildren are following Christ.[11]

Like Norm, many people have experienced a family of origin that was less than desirable. The pain of the past may differ, in both type and degree, from one person to the next, but the impact is deeply felt in every case. The haunting and poisoning effect of bad memories and abusive relationships can stay with us for a long time, often subconsciously. We must deal with past negatives openly and honestly. It is imperative. I suggest it's best to do so with help that is both professionally competent and biblically based.

There is hope for those who grew up in hurtful families: When you come to Christ, you actually enter into a whole new family. That wonderful new family in Christ has its own past, its own heritage, and its own glorious future. Our faith in Christ becomes "the assurance of things hoped for."[12] We come to God believing "that He is and that He is a rewarder of those who seek Him. . . . Therefore, . . . [we] lay aside every encumbrance and the sin which so easily entangles us, . . . fixing our eyes on Jesus, the author and perfecter of faith."[13]

All the while, we continue to look toward the home and heritage "whose architect and builder is God."[14] Wow! You can do this, in the power of Christ.

> BY GOD'S GRACE, DETERMINE TO WALK A DIFFERENT PATH YOURSELF AND TO PASS ALONG A DIFFERENT HERITAGE TO THOSE WHO WILL COME BEHIND YOU.

Don't spend a lot of time fretting over a missing heritage you never got from your family. Don't waste time casting blame. That *never* helps. Be realistic, and accept the reality of your timeline past. But by God's grace, determine to walk a different path yourself and to pass along a different heritage to those who will come behind you.

Three of the four most beautiful women in my immediate family have had to set aside some painful elements from the past. And they've done it in spades. My wife and two of my three daughters-in-law come from broken homes. In some cases, there was abuse, in some abandonment, and in some both. Some of the memories are quite painful, but these wonderful ladies have not let the past hold them back. And in every case, the key has been the same—a personal relationship with Jesus Christ.

One past event (Christ's sacrifice on their behalf), coupled with a present personal decision (to accept Christ as their Savior), changed the future altogether (for themselves and for their families).

Like my great-grandparents and my friend Norm, they've chosen to believe in Jesus and to identify with him and *his* legacy. Consequently, they have an altogether new identity and have been grafted into the magnificent heritage of the King of kings.

I have another friend who has determined to overcome his past and to become the pivotal generation in his family. He came from a dysfunctional home where living for the moment was the norm. Addictions, rampant sexuality, adultery, and drugs were commonplace in his home of origin. He saw the poor choices that had wounded his parents and destroyed his siblings, and he determined he would do it differently.

He married a woman of character, and together they raised their new family. As his sons were entering their early adulthood years, it was clear that they had become young men of character, purpose, and Christian commitment. When the day came for his youngest son to leave home for college, the two men stood beside each other. Dad's heart was remembering. It had been a long haul, but it was clear that the next generation had taken root in good soil. He turned to his son, and with deep emotion, spoke these words: "Finally, the family name has something to be proud of."

COMING TO YOUR TRUE HERITAGE

We all long for a home and a heritage, something to be proud of. We thirst to belong, and God has given us that very thirst in order to draw us to himself. The Bible teaches emphatically that in order for us to be "at home" with God, we have to know him personally. Stands to reason, doesn't it?

How do we come to know God personally? We know him through his Son, Jesus Christ.

Let me explain by using an example from my own past. Until I was a college student, I had never traveled east of Idaho. But during those college days I got to spend a glorious week vacationing in beautiful New England. I stayed with a prominent family with significant connections to Harvard, to Boston's financial centers, and to American big business. As I recall, they were actually related to more than one of the passengers on the *Mayflower.* Talk about heritage!

I slept, ate, played, and fellowshipped for that week in their historic old home, which had been built sometime in the late 1600s or early 1700s. Beautifully restored and refurbished, the home and its heritage were overwhelming to me. I was actually touching artifacts from the earliest days of our nation's history! If memory serves me correctly, the primitive glass panes in the front door dated from 1680. Near the old central fireplace rested an infant cradle from Plymouth Colony. It was one of only two in existence. I felt so incredibly blessed to stay in such a stately home.

As you can imagine, the home was magnificent, but the family was even more so. Kind and unselfish, generous and humble, they treated me like one of their own. I felt entirely at home. I belonged.

Here's the question for your consideration: How in the world did a coal miner's kid from the West Coast (who didn't even know the name of his own great-grandfather at the time) come to feel so welcome in a historic home occupied by a family that traced its ancestry to the very roots of America?

The answer is really pretty simple. I was so readily accepted there because I had a personal relationship with the family's son. I knew him. He was my friend and my roommate, and he wanted to take me home for a visit. He was my ticket. I was identified with him. He had invited me home with him, and I had accepted his invitation. By virtue of my close relationship to him, I was treated as a member of the family. Makes better sense now, doesn't it?

The same thing is true of my home in heaven. One of these days, death will knock on my door, and I will step off the timeline. I will move to another home, a home of incredible heritage and glory. I will move from this worn, old house (my body) on this beat-up, old planet (Earth) to a whole new world of wonder all because of my personal relationship with the Son.

> ONE OF THESE DAYS, DEATH WILL KNOCK ON MY DOOR, AND I WILL STEP OFF THE TIMELINE. I WILL MOVE TO ANOTHER HOME, A HOME OF INCREDIBLE HERITAGE AND GLORY.

That's the way heaven works. How are you and I going to gain entrance to God's heaven? There's only one way: through a personal relationship with the Son. The only way that any one of us sinful earthlings is ever going to get to heaven is by accepting the invitation of heaven's Son to come home with him—and for more than a visit!

God's Word describes three basic steps for accepting the Son's invitation:

1. You and I have to admit we're sinners who cannot live up to God's standard of perfection. "All have sinned and fall short of the glory of God."[15] Therefore, we don't *deserve* to live with God. "The wages of sin is death, but the gift of God is eternal life in Christ Jesus our Lord."[16]
2. You and I have to acknowledge that Jesus is God's only Son and that he died on the cross to pay the penalty for our sins. And that he rose from the grave three days later in complete victory over death. "Christ died for our sins according to the Scriptures, ... he was buried, ... [and] he was raised on the third day according to the Scriptures."[17] "If you confess with your mouth, 'Jesus is Lord,' and believe in your heart that God raised him from the dead, you will be saved."[18]
3. We have to believe these things personally, in mind and heart,

and depend on Christ alone, never our own works, as the only source of salvation. "There is salvation in no one else; for there is no other name under heaven that has been given among men by which we must be saved."[19] "By grace you have been saved through faith; and that not of yourselves, *it is* the gift of God; not as a result of works, so that no one may boast."[20] "'Whoever will call on the name of the Lord will be saved.'"[21]

If you've never accepted Christ as your Savior, do it now. Don't think it's hard to talk to God. Don't fret about your lack of experience praying. Don't worry about the vocabulary you should use. God understands the intention of your heart. He knows genuine repentance and faith when he sees it. Just be real and genuine with him. Take hold of the heritage offered to you by God's Son, the High King of heaven.

Now then, if you've just accepted Christ as your Savior, I say to you, "Welcome home, Cinderella." You'll never have to fear the stroke of midnight again. You may have felt like the ugly stepsister in the past. No longer. You're now a genuine member of the forever family. All you have to do now is grow in Christ. That, in and of itself, will give you a legacy worth passing along to those who come behind you.[22]

That's quite a heritage, wouldn't you say? You are being fitted together with your new Christian family, the body of Christ, his church. You will discover, with every passing day, something new and rich about your glorious past, present, and future in Christ.

You have a new birthright in Christ, and it can never be taken from you. You're at home—really at home—and you belong. Now pass the heritage on.

And then one day, perhaps not far from now, when history has reached its glorious climax, we'll go home, you and me, to the dream residence we've always longed for. Cinderella is going home to the palace forever. We've been homesick for Eden for a long time now, but it's just around the corner, one step beyond the timeline.

Your Journey on the Timeline

Impact Statement: No matter where you are on the timeline, build from there.

Summary

- Roots are crucial to living things, and human beings are no exception.
- It's axiomatic: The healthiest individuals are those from the healthiest families. That's the way roots work.
- The roots that matter most have nothing to do with prominence, fame, or material wealth. The healthiest roots are matters of character.
- Genealogies matter. In Adam, all die. So, in Christ, all are made alive.
- If you can't find much that's positive in your roots, devote yourself to becoming the pivotal generation. Start the line that your descendants can be proud of.
- Where you can, create an heirloom, an honest tribute to your spiritual roots.

Key Questions

1. Can you trace a spiritual root in your family history? Did it come down to you through your parents? an aunt or uncle? your grandparents? What is the spiritual influence in your heritage?
2. Are the lessons to be learned from your heritage more from contrast than acceptance? Does your family heritage teach you more about what *not* to do than what to do? Is the family legacy more negative than positive? If so, will you resolve to become the pivotal generation in your family line?
3. Have you considered what you want your own epitaph to say?

Moving Forward

After completing enough research to whet your appetite, make plans to visit—preferably with other family members—the graves of some of your ancestors, especially those most worthy of emulation. Thank God for them. Resolve to avoid the poor choices of other ancestors whose lives are less worthy of emulation. Put your resolve in writing. Leave a record for those who will follow you.

GAINING PERSPECTIVE

Sometimes when we're reading the Bible, it's easy to forget that the people portrayed there are actual flesh-and-blood human beings, just like us. The farther we look back on the timeline, the more unreal these individuals can seem. When we read about someone such as Abraham, for example, who is called "the friend of God" and who had numerous visions of the Almighty during his lifetime, it all seems just a bit beyond our grasp.

But it really doesn't matter that some of these people lived four thousand years ago, or that their names and their stories have been captured for the ages in the Bible. Flesh is flesh, and blood is blood. Abraham put his sandals on one foot at a time, just as we would.

Why is this important? Well, because God teaches us truths about himself—and about ourselves—through the lives of people on the time-line past. The more we understand the lives of these people and their relationships with God, the more we will understand our own lives and our relationships with God.

Let's look for a moment at a very human event in Abraham's life; during the days when he was still known as Abram, before God changed his name. It was a time of real fear, when his life seemed to be slipping away from him; a time when Abram had an extraordinary experience; a time when God lifted him up high above the timeline for a priceless glimpse at the entirety of his life.

> "TRULY, TRULY, I SAY TO YOU, BEFORE ABRAHAM WAS BORN, I AM."
> — JOHN 8:58, NASB

• • •

Abram was afraid—desperately afraid, with that sickening sense that the very earth beneath his feet was caving in beneath him.

Everything he had been leaning on since he had left his home, his job, and his friends and family back in Ur seemed to be slip-sliding away. What was his life really all about? He had reached a juncture in his life where he was filled with doubt, disappointment, and anxiety. Perhaps he was nursing a secret sorrow. It had no doubt been building in his heart for months—maybe even years. And now, for whatever reason, it had come to a head.

What was he to do with all those promises about a child? God had spoken with such certainty. He had been so specific. And now . . . ? His wife, Sarai, was still barren—as barren now at ninety as she had been at twenty-one. Abram knew that his own body had left the procreation phase somewhere in the long decades past. Now it seemed clear that he and Sarai would only grow older and feebler until they finally passed away, and Abram's heir would be Eliezer of Damascus, a servant in his household.

Had the Lord failed him? No, more likely he had failed the Lord somehow, he figured, and now he was reaping the consequences of a less-than-perfect life.

Just about that time, God picked up his discouraged servant and took him for a ride over the timeline.

MY RIDE, AND WHERE IT TOOK ME

Have you ever been there? Has God ever lifted you above your life for a moment or two, giving you a "big picture" glimpse and helping you to see your years on the planet in the wider context of past, present, and future?

In the Introduction to this book, I mentioned my near-death experience in the heat and confusion of combat in Vietnam. Confronted with the prospect of my own death, I began a pilgrimage that continues to this very day. Having been face-to-face with the very real possibility of dying, I began to wonder, *Why am I alive? Why have others died, but I haven't? Why am I over here in the jungles of Vietnam while many of my peers are protesting the war or heading for Canada? What's going on?*

The questions kept coming, one on top of another. *What really matters in life? Okay, so I've been allowed to live while some of my fellow soldiers died. What then do I do with this life that's been given back to me?*

Suddenly—or so it seemed—I was on a military transport, headed for Hawaii to meet my wife on R & R. Flying into Honolulu was almost surreal for me. Plucked out of the blood and dirt and fear of a world at war and onto a plane, I stepped into a paradise of peace and rest. The gentle trade winds caressed my face. The people around me were laughing, relaxed, immersed in the details of having a good time. Didn't they know that men were fighting for their lives, fighting and dying for the very survival of a nation just across the ocean?

Which was real—the hell in Vietnam or the paradise of Oahu? How could those two realities possibly coexist in the same universe? The juxtaposition in space and time—from war one day to the arms of my wife and baby son the next—was mind-boggling.

In those moments of internal crosscurrents and stress, I sensed God lifting me gently up over my timeline. Looking down on where I was, where I had been, and where I might be, some answers began to emerge from the fog. The answer to "what matters?" and "why am I alive?" began to take shape. Here's what I saw in those precious moments of clarity: *I'm alive for two primary reasons: my bride and my kids, and God's bride and his kids. My family and his family.* What else is there? Really, everything else is a diversion at best. The only things that will last forever are God and his people.

> IN THOSE MOMENTS OF INTERNAL CROSS-CURRENTS AND STRESS, I SENSED GOD LIFTING ME GENTLY UP OVER MY TIMELINE.

Those memorable hours on that Polynesian beach, holding Linda and watching Kent—in total contrast to the dark experience in the Dak Poko Valley—became anchors for my soul, milestones on my timeline.

Out of mist and haze, a plan began to form. Steps began to clarify. I moved from being a soldier in one kingdom, serving my beloved nation, to being a soldier in another kingdom, serving my beloved King—all of which pretty much explains why I am in vocational ministry to this day.

I think Abram experienced something similar in Genesis 15.

Let's try to view this story in a fresh way. Imagine the Lord and Abram standing on a high bluff at sunset, overlooking a valley that is bisected by a long highway stretching for many miles in either direction. This is Abram's timeline—and the timeline beyond.

THE TIMELINE PRESENT

Can you see it? God places his hand on Abram's shoulder and gestures straight down to a point on the highway directly below. This is Abram's present, and God has something to say about the state of affairs at that very moment.

> "Do not be afraid, Abram. I am your shield, your exceedingly great reward."[1]

In effect, God is saying, "Remember who I am, my child, and you will know better who you are. Right now, in this very moment, I am your shield. I am your exceedingly great reward. *That* is reality."

You wouldn't think we would need a supernatural perspective to see our present circumstances, would you? I mean, after all, we *live* in the present. To look into the past, yes, it's easy to see how a little divine help might enable us to see what we had missed in the years gone by. And looking into the future? Well, that certainly would require being elevated over the timeline, a perspective that is impossible within our human limitations. *But the present?* Do we need heaven's assistance to see where we are?

Yes, we do, because most of the time we don't realize where we are. We can't see where we're standing. We fail to comprehend our opportunities. We don't value what we possess. We don't understand what we really need—and what we don't need at all. We can't begin to tally our resources, and we have little idea of our peril. And as to living in the present, it may be like living in a house of a thousand rooms. We may see what is immediately around us, but what else is happening in this moment on the timeline that completely bypasses our awareness?

> MOST OF THE TIME WE DON'T REALIZE WHERE WE ARE. WE CAN'T SEE WHERE WE'RE STANDING. WE DON'T UNDERSTAND WHAT WE REALLY NEED—AND WHAT WE DON'T NEED AT ALL.

We're like Elisha's servant, Gehazai, who despaired to observe the Aramean soldiers surrounding the city of Dothan but didn't have eyes to see the heavenly armies surrounding the Arameans.[2] We're like the half-healed blind man, who said, "I see people; they look like trees walking around."[3] We see life with only the vaguest apprehension of reality, "a poor reflection as in a mirror."[4]

Abram, disheartened, weary, and anxious, had lost sight of what he had in the moment. He had a God who called him *friend*. He had a Lord who declared himself Abram's shield. And he needed to be reminded that his relationship with the living God, the Creator of the universe, was a very, very great reward.

THE TIMELINE FUTURE

If you can still picture God and Abram standing on that imaginary bluff, looking far down at the highway below, imagine the Lord nudging Abram and pointing off into the horizon of the future.

> "Now look toward the heavens, and count the stars, if you are able to count them. . . . So shall your descendants be."[5]

Far down that timeline highway, beyond the setting sun and into a purple horizon, God shows Abram what he could never see beyond his present "hopeless" situation—a vast field of stars, like dust. "Those are your children, Abram, and your grandchildren and their children and out into generations innumerable." Abram's mind was focused on the promise of a single child; God lifted him above the timeline to show him *nations* of descendants.

That's the way it is with you and me, of course. We can't see the forest for the trees. We walk through life with reading glasses on our noses, enabling us to see the problems and heartaches close-up but rendering God's promises out ahead of us an indecipherable blur. We're so troubled by our present that we forget the wondrous future that awaits us just a little ways down the timeline and beyond:

> "For I know the plans I have for you," declares the LORD, "plans to prosper you and not to harm you, plans to give you hope and a future."[6]

In my opinion whatever we may have to go through now is less than nothing compared with the magnificent future God has planned for us. The whole creation is on tiptoe to see the wonderful sight of the sons of God coming into their own.[7]

Dear friends, we are already God's children, but he has not yet shown us what we will be like when Christ appears. But we do know that we will be like him, for we will see him as he really is.[8]

Do not fear, little flock, for it is your Father's good pleasure to give you the kingdom.[9]

C. S. Lewis writes that the first two words we will say after we open our eyes in heaven will be, "Of course." *Now I understand. Now I see. Now it makes sense. Now it all comes together.*

While Abram was still up and above his little portion of the timeline, God had him look to his left down the timeline highway—into his own recent past.

"'I am the LORD who brought you out of Ur of the Chaldeans, to give you this land to possess it.'"[10]

"Remember, Abram? Remember how it was? Remember how I came into your life, claimed you for my own, and led you on a journey where your feet had never walked before?"

A friend of mine was talking to a missionary recently who told him about leading a Muslim friend to Christ. Years later, he heard that man give his testimony, and he was somewhat stunned to hear a string of events leading up to that salvation event—things his friend had never told him. The man spoke of walking the streets of Kabul as a young boy and picking up a piece of paper. The paper talked about Jesus and salvation and eternal life, and the boy never forgot that. It was the first of many steps leading him to that moment when the missionary presented the full plan of salvation and the man bowed his head to receive Jesus.

The Muslim convert had not told the missionary those stories because he hadn't even remembered them himself. But some time after he had turned to Christ, the Lord took him on a little journey back down his timeline, showing him things he hadn't thought of for years. "You see," the Lord was telling him, "I have always loved you, and I was there all along, calling you to myself."

BACK TO THE FUTURE

Still on that high bluff, far above the timeline, God gently turned Abram once again to look into the future.

> "Know for certain that your descendants will be strangers in a land that is not theirs, where they will be enslaved and oppressed four hundred years. But I will also judge the nation whom they will serve, and afterward they will come out with many possessions. As for you, you shall go to your fathers in peace; you will be buried at a good old age. Then in the fourth generation they will return here, for the iniquity of the Amorite is not yet complete."[11]

In that one conversation, the Lord lifted his servant Abram up above the timeline to show him what is, what was, and what will be. God would later lift another beloved servant of his above the timeline, a man named John, and give him a similar view.

> "I am the Alpha and the Omega ... who is and who was and who is to come, the Almighty.... Therefore write the things which you have seen, and the things which are, and the things which will take place after these things."[12]

How important is this declaration of God's eternalness and his supremacy over time? It must be important enough to be declared continually before the throne of heaven forever and ever.

In John's vision, he saw "four living creatures," each with "six wings and ... covered with eyes all around, even under his wings. Day and night they never stop saying: 'Holy, holy, holy is the Lord God Almighty, *who was, and is, and is to come.*'"[13]

The Bible says that Abram believed the Lord after that little ride over the timeline. But wouldn't you know it? In the very next chapter of Genesis, Abram and Sarai's faith fails again, and they cobble together a plan to produce an heir through their own earthly methods.

Abram and Sarai were real people who had their highs of great faith and their lows of doubt and fear. Even so, Abram had been for a ride over the timeline—as the Lord may very well do for you and me in a moment of supernatural insight and clarity. I think we can be sure the old patriarch never forgot those moments of elevation and understanding.

And neither will we.

YOUR JOURNEY ON THE TIMELINE
Impact Statement: We gain perspective when God lifts us above the timeline.

SUMMARY

- People in the Bible are just flesh-and-blood people—no matter when they walked on the earth.
- God will give his perspective on life to those who seek it.
- A big-picture view of life includes the past, present, and future.
- Seasons of great trial or trauma in our lives, when we come to the end of ourselves and are utterly cast upon the Lord and his grace, may be the very times when God will give us a view of our wider timelines.
- We need the assistance of heaven to understand our present circumstances every bit as much as we need that help to consider our past and future.
- We become so troubled by our present situations that we forget the wondrous future waiting for us just a little ways down the timeline and beyond.

KEY QUESTIONS

1. Have you experienced a moment in your life when God gave you a wider view of where you've been, where you are, and where you're headed? Was it a reassurance or a warning?
2. How is it possible that God could show us *new things* as we consider our past?

3. Why do we need to be reminded—even on a daily basis—of who God is, what God has done, and what God has promised?

4. Why is it so important for the book of Revelation to repeat over and over that our Lord is someone "who was, and is, and is to come"?

5. After such a glorious revelation of the timeline in Genesis 15, how do you explain Abram and Sarai's going back to makeshift human solutions in Genesis 16?

MOVING FORWARD

As a part of your daily prayer time, ask the Lord for the gift of perspective on your life, and then wait with anticipation for what he will show you. He has promised to give us wisdom when we ask him in faith.[14]

1 3

THE END IS ONLY
THE BEGINNING

The timeline is finite.

We talk about "ancient history" and the "distant future" as if the timeline stretched endlessly both ways. But it doesn't. It's a fixed line, with a point marking its beginning and a corresponding point marking its terminus.

Carl Sagan and his evolutionist friends may speak confidently and expansively of "billions and billions" of years, but I don't buy it. The way I read the Bible, this whole divine venture of a material universe and the creation and redemption of man is a rather brief enterprise. Just a blip of something called *time*—a hyphen between two eternities.

But even if the evolutionists were right about the numberless aeons before the notorious Big Bang, the timeline would still be very, very brief. A faint pencil mark on the Great Wall of China. A bit of straw floating in the Pacific. An eyelash in deep space. Compared to the eternity so near at hand, time itself is a heartbeat, a sigh, a single tick of the cosmic clock.

It's tragic when young soldiers fall in battle, when the good die young, or when death claims someone in their middle years, before they have a chance to hold their grandchildren or savor the fruit of their labors. God never minimizes such sorrow, as our Lord demonstrated when he encountered the widow of Nain, stumbling along in a funeral procession beside the casket of her only son. The Gospel writer tells us that "when the Lord saw her, his heart went out to her and he said, 'Don't cry.' Then he went up and touched the coffin, and those carrying it stood still. He said, 'Young man, I say to you, get up!' The dead man sat up and began to talk, and Jesus gave him back to his mother."[1]

> IF OUR LIVES ARE BRIEF, SO IS THE ENTIRE TIMELINE; OUR YEARS IN THE SUN ARE LITTLE MORE THAN A HAIRLINE SCRATCH ON THAT LINE.

But just a short while later, that young man would die again. His timeline started, stopped, and then started again; but inevitably, it also stopped again. Even though he was touched by the Lord of life, he remained mortal, like the rest of us.

If our lives are brief, so is the entire timeline; our years in the sun are little more than a hairline scratch on that line.

Ah, but the timeline is not the complete story. Everything changed when the Lord of time entered time, bringing word of life *outside* of time. The Great Shepherd said of his sheep, "I give them eternal life, and they shall never perish; no one can snatch them out of my hand."[2] Pouring out his heart in prayer to the Father, the Son of God said, "Father, I want these whom you have given me to be with me where I am. Then they can see all the glory you gave me because you loved me even before the world began!"[3]

The timeline begins and ends, and because we're creatures of time, our fractions of the timeline also begin and end. But the God who entered time will take us with him outside of time. Because of Jesus, the perishable will put on imperishability, and the mortal will put on immortality.

> *For I know that my Redeemer lives,*
> *And He shall stand at last on the earth;*
> *And after my skin is destroyed, this I know,*
> *That in my flesh I shall see God,*
> *Whom I shall see for myself,*
> *And my eyes shall behold, and not another.* [4]

Our timelines will end, perhaps today, perhaps tomorrow, perhaps in fifty years. But in ending, they will begin again. History will become eternity, death will be swallowed up in life, and our lives will last as long as the life of the one who can never die.

● ● ●

The old plaque over the fireplace reads, "There's no place like home." Enough said. It's at home that we have the best chance of being fully . . . well, at home. Accepted. Settled. Secure. Protected. Alive. It is at home that we know and are known. Sounds like heaven. Actually, it is. Heaven will be home at last. But that's getting just a tad ahead of the story. . . .

When we started this book together, I was sitting on the couch with my grandson watching *The Lion King.* You remember the story. The happy kingdom, ruled by the good Mufasa was blessed with abundant grass, sparkling streams, and healthy animals. But the kingdom was usurped from its rightful ruler by the wicked schemes of the evil Scar. Under the tyrannical rule

> "AT THAT TIME I WILL GATHER YOU; AT THAT TIME I WILL BRING YOU HOME."
> —ZEPHANIAH 3:20, NIV

of the narcissistic Scar, the citizens lived in horror and pain as evil had had its way. The once glorious kingdom deteriorated to the point of being unrecognizable. But in time, the young lion prince returned to the kingdom. He defeated the evil one, removed the usurper from the throne, and returned the kingdom to its once glorious state, presumably to live happily ever after.

The parallels to the basic theme of the Bible are clear. Paradise, once lost, is regained. We will, one day, return to our roots.

Planet Earth, once a paradise where God and man walked together in the cool of the day, has been taken over by the evil adversary, Satan, "the prince of the power of the air."[5] But heaven's King will not let it stand. The usurper will be defeated. Two thousand years ago, the Lamb of God came to earth to deal with the destructive power of sin. At Calvary, Christ fought the D–Day battle that ensured the final outcome of the war. With the passing of every day since, earth is that much closer to its consummation and Christ's ultimate victory.

Soon, Christ will return as the Lion of Judah to restore the throne and resurrect the kingdom to its once glorious state. And, guaranteed, his people will live happily ever after. Paradise, once lost, will be regained.

Yes, upon a day yet future, the earth will fulfill the purpose for which it was created. Isaiah, the prince of prophets, stated it most clearly: "'Holy, Holy, Holy, is the LORD of hosts, the whole earth is full of His glory.'"[6] Some contend that the final phrase should be translated, "The fullness of the whole earth is His glory."

Earth will come full circle to fully realize God's original intent. And when earth is resurrected to its fullness, we will see the glory of God as he intended. The story of the earth's redemptive restoration is no Disney fantasy. It is true history. It is the story of stories. It is *the* story to be remembered, and it will be remembered forever. The Bible indicates that this story of stories will be memorialized forever by two things: Jesus' eternal humanity and his nail–scarred hands.

> THOSE WHO LOVE JESUS CHRIST AS SAVIOR WILL BE FOREVER AT HOME WITH THE LORD. AT HOME! AT PEACE. FOREVER.

Think about it. We'll be free at last! Those who love Jesus Christ as Savior will be forever at home with the Lord. At home! At peace. Forever. The longing for home that constantly percolates in every one of us will be realized. That's worth remembering. And it brings us full circle—your past shapes your future, and your future motivates your present.

Nurtured memories form the baseline of our identities and the foundation of our futures. At no time is this more true than when we think of heaven as our future home. Our past on this earth has allowed us to be introduced to Christ. Our decision for Christ in the past governs our behavior in the present and guarantees our future in heaven with him. So our thirst for heaven is really the ultimate reflection of our Creator-ingrained longings for home.

BACK TO THE FUTURE . . . AND YOUR DREAM HOME

Frederick Buechner, an award-winning writer and a very thoughtful man, writes of a season in his life at college when he was both especially busy and especially lonely—scurrying here, scurrying there, keeping the car in repair, clothes clean, and the refrigerator stocked. It was hard to find stillness. It was hard to be at home.

> Somewhere around the time of that Harvard winter I dreamed I was staying in a hotel. I had a wonderful room where all was well with me and I was at peace. Then I left the hotel for some reason, and when I returned, I tried to get the same room back except that I did not know where it was in the hotel. If it had a number, I didn't remember it. The man at the desk said he knew exactly the room I meant. He said all I had to do was ask for it by name. Then he told me the name. He said the name of the room where I had been at peace was Remember.
>
> I think of all the things you and I could remember that would not bring us peace at all, but I believe that at least part of what the dream meant was that way beyond all those things, at the innermost heart, at the farthest reach, of our remembering, there is peace. The secret place of the Most High is there. Eden is there, the still waters, the green pastures. Home is there.[7]

Dreams and peace and home. Seems like they belong together, doesn't it? When after a lifetime of scurrying after things large and small, we finally begin to slow down, to be still, to be reflective—remembering—that's when we all somehow end up coming back home, at least deep down inside, in our souls. A wise person once said, "The world is round, and the place which may seem like the end may also be the beginning."[8] Sure enough, the tide that carried us out to sea in our youth is also the tide that turns and brings us back again in our old age, full circle. It's time to come full circle on this book. So let's finish where we started. At home . . . remembering.

We come by our longings for home quite naturally. God put it there. It's engraved on our souls by our Creator. He invented our present home, planet Earth, and he intended for us to enjoy it to the full—no pain, sorrow, or disappointment, only full-on peace, joy, togetherness, and belonging. Totally at home.

It sure hasn't turned out that way, has it? As it is right now, this old house, planet Earth, is more than a bit run-down. Worse than that, it has been abused by an evil slumlord, and it has been "lived in" by a bunch of wild and crazy sinners—us. Planet Earth, like the pridelands surrounding Pride Rock, is showing severe wear and tear.

To be sure, this old house has moved well beyond being a fixer-upper. In fact, it pretty much looks as if what it needs is complete demolition and starting over. And that is precisely the plan, God's plan. He's going to melt this old planet down, and then he's going to take the raw material, shape it as only he can, and make it perfect. It will be a brand-new earth. And, as you well know, God has the resources to pull it off.

MELTDOWN

Listen to God tell the story in his own words, as recorded by the apostle Peter: "The heavens will pass away with a roar and the elements will be destroyed with intense heat, and the earth and its works will be burned up."[9]

God, at that point, will call in the chips on that old usurper Satan. "Hold it. Stop right there. Enough!" Time and sin and corruption have had their way with this old earth for long enough. "By the word of God the heavens existed long ago and the earth was formed out of water. . . . But by His word the present heavens and earth are being reserved for fire."[10]

> THE HEAVENS WILL PASS AWAY WITH A ROAR AND THE ELEMENTS WILL BE DESTROYED WITH INTENSE HEAT, AND THE EARTH AND ITS WORKS WILL BE BURNED UP.
>
> —2 PETER 3:10, NASB

Because God is patient and desires that people should respond to him, he has held off that coming judgment day. But he will not hold it off forever. Still, the really good news is that the demolition of this existing planet is not the end of all things. God has some plans: "According to His promise we are looking for new heavens and a new earth, in which righteousness dwells."[11]

God is going to call a time-out, and he'll order one huge "do over." Earth, our home, will experience the mother of all makeovers. Earth is right in the center of God's eternal plans. As a matter of fact, earth is going to be resurrected, redeemed, and more than remade, from the ground up. Even the ground itself (make that earth) is going to be remade. I'm so looking forward to my new home on the New Earth! And you will too. The dream home, the one for which you have longed all your life, is just ahead.

Again, let God tell the story, as recorded by the apostle John:

> Then I saw a new heaven and a new earth; for the first heaven and the first earth passed away. . . . And I heard a loud voice from the throne, saying, "Behold, the tabernacle [home!] of God is among men, and He will dwell [be at home] among them, and they shall be His people, and God Himself will be among them, and He will wipe away every tear from their eyes; and there will no longer be any death . . . mourning, or crying, or pain; the first things have passed away."[12]

God, at home, with us. Emmanuel to the fullest. The cool of the day will again provide time for walks with God. Man, we will be at home with him! As the glorious song says, "God and man at table are sat down." Free from sin, fully at peace, home, at last, forever. Our roots will be realized. Yes, our lifelong longings for a real home will be fulfilled. Our dream home will come true.

My friend Randy Alcorn says it well:

I used to say "When we get to Heaven we'll be going home for the first time." I spoke of the paradox of how our true home is a place we've never been. I've since revised this statement because it's misleading. The Bible teaches that our eternal home will be a place we've already been—earth. True, it will be a New Earth, a transformed earth. . . . Human beings were made from earth, have always lived on earth, are geared to find pleasure in the things of earth. If we think of Heaven only as the realm where angels live, there's a real problem. We were not made from the angelic realm, nor for it. . . . There's one place that qualifies as the only home we've ever known—earth. It's the home God made for us. . . . Revelation 21 makes it clear—it's the New Earth. . . . Our home will seem new and fresh and we'll feel like we're there for the first time, yet it will be familiar because our home will be a much-improved version of the world we grew up on.[13]

Yes, every person, to one degree or another, has a longing for home. We all know something of "homesickness." One Christian, on a cross-country flight to his childhood hometown, Chicago, describes a sensation common to all of us:

There's not much left of my childhood haunts. After my father died, the family sold the home in which I grew up. . . . Old neighbors have moved away. And today is a difficult journey. I'm returning to visit my mother, who's dying of cancer. If the doctors are right, she has only a short time to live.

My warm feelings about home, though, will inevitably live on even after her death. I suspect I will always be homesick for the place that continues to exist only in my memories. My heart will be forever tugged toward the neighborhood where my parents nurtured me and where my childhood unfolded. . . . Homesickness . . . is a topic that resonates deeply.[14]

Homesickness will always resonate deeply in this life. The homesickness we experience on this earth will never be completely cured this side of glory. Our Creator intended that we never be fully at home apart from his full presence. Call that heaven on earth. All that is good about our present home is merely a shadow, a small foretaste of the home we were made for—the New Earth. The continuity between this present life and our future finds its roots in our true house.

In one sense, as Randy Alcorn says, the irony is that our true home is a place we've never been. Yet, we *have* been there because "there" is *here*—planet Earth. Still, living on this fallen, twisted version of our God-made home leaves us longing for deliverance. Sometimes, in our weaker moments, we may think that in heaven we'll miss "the good things" of this earth. But, of course, we won't. We'll have all the good things of this earth—and then some. Forever.

The New Earth will be all the good with none of the bad. Can you imagine walking and exploring familiar places with both your great-grandparents and your great-grandchildren? All to the glory of Christ!

HOMEWARD BOUND

We're homeward bound, but we're not there yet. That's why this world, as it now is, can never truly be called our home. That's why God's people will always experience this life more or less as strangers or exiles. The Bible says as much:

All these died in faith, without receiving the promises, but having seen them and having welcomed them from a distance, and having confessed that they were strangers and exiles on the earth. For those who say such things make it clear that they are seeking a country of their own. . . . They desire a better country, that is, a heavenly one. Therefore God is not ashamed to be called their God; for He has prepared a city for them.[15]

What are the "promises" these people saw and welcomed from a distance, but did not receive? What is this "better country" they desired? It is the home for which we were made, the home for which the earth itself was originally made, and it is the home which this earth will one day—yet to come—become again, the New Earth. Then it will truly be heaven on earth. God wants his children to be at home, and he has promised us that one day we will be.

And remember, right now, as you read these words, God's own Son, a carpenter by trade, has gone to "prepare a place for you."[16]

Yes, God's people are a people of place.

• • •

In my opinion, well-meaning Christians too often tend to spiritualize heaven away. Oh, they believe it's real and good and where God dwells. But somehow they conclude it's not spiritual to think of heaven as an actual location. It seems too familiar somehow—too material, too earthly.

But heaven truly is a place. In fact, it's the place of all places. And I believe it will be familiar.

The Bible consistently highlights the notion of a homeland as a *good* thing. Yes, our sin has turned our earthly home into a shadow of its former (and future) self. We have moved, for the time being, east of Eden. One author (unknown to me) said it well: "We have been lost and wandering since we left Eden, wandering the world, looking for home, and getting

> "WE HAVE BEEN LOST AND WANDERING SINCE WE LEFT EDEN, WANDERING THE WORLD, LOOKING FOR HOME, AND GETTING MIGHTY DIRTY IN THE PROCESS."
> —AUTHOR UNKNOWN

mighty dirty in the process." That's the bad news. But there's also some very good news: When our Lord redeems this broken world, we will at last be home. Paradise will be regained. The new heaven and the new earth will be the dream home come true. Until then, we can see it from a distance.

The longing for home is in our Father's heavenly gene pool. And it's all spelled out in his Word, the Bible. The nineteenth century poet, John Greenleaf Whittier, described our wandering and returning:

> We search the world for good. We cull
> The bright, the great, the beautiful.
> And weary seekers of the best,
> We come home laden from our quest,
> And find that all the sages said,
> Was in the book our mothers read.

"The climax of history," writes Randy Alcorn, "will be the creation of new heavens and a new Earth, a resurrected universe inhabited by resurrected people. . . . We will live on a planet so much like this one that it is called 'the New Earth' . . . Our ancestors came from Eden. Something in us has never forgotten that."[17]

I believe Randy is right. Our eternal home will be "remarkably like the original place for human beings—the earth."[18] Madeleine L'Engle would likely agree. She writes, "We are, I believe, given glimpses of heaven (here on earth) and I have had a few. Walking down a dirt road on a shining summer day, I moved into a realm of beauty and depth that became indescribable once I had left it, but it gives me a hint that after I die I may say, 'Oh glory! What a thin way of living I have just left!'"[19]

Because I agree that the New Earth will be a glorious restoration of earth as we know it, it is not at all difficult for me to dream, with some measure of biblical confidence, of my revisiting (for a very long and delicious time) the transformed Teanaway River, where I swam as a child. I dream of climbing to the peak of the refurbished Stuart Range, where so much imaginary childhood adventure took place for me. I imagine swapping campfire stories with fellow pilgrims about how wonderfully God has brought his forever family home.

Like the saints mentioned in Hebrews 11, I, too, *look forward* (v. 10) with a strong *longing for* that *better country* (v. 16), that *city prepared for us by God* (v. 16). I, too, look forward to the *things promised* (v. 13)—a transformed, resurrected New Earth, fresh from the hand of God himself—a New Earth both fresh and familiar, the earth I have known, but far, far better, as God originally intended.

God is not a frustrated mad scientist, a Gyro Gearloose, whose laboratory floor is strewn with one failed experiment after another. God does not quit and walk away. He finishes, or redeems, what he starts. When it comes to the earth, God has not forgotten his original intention. Nor should we.

> *Goin' home, I'm always goin' home inside.*
> *There's an ache in my heart*
> *That I can't bear.*
> *Take me home, take my hand and lead me home*
> *Oh Lord*
> *I'm so broken up inside*
> *I need to hide in your love, in your hand,*
> *So take me home.*[20]

Until Jesus comes to take you home, keep on remembering all the ways he has been good to you, to your family, and to your nation. Remembering is the most profitable exercise you'll ever do—the art of nurturing your family's hope, love, and values across the timeline.

Your nurtured memories are the baseline of the future, both in this life and the one to come.

Remember.

Impact Statement: The end of the timeline is only the beginning.

SUMMARY

- God created the earth and humankind to enjoy fellowship together with him forever.
- Planet Earth has been abused by an evil slumlord, Satan, and it has been torn to shreds by a bunch of wild and crazy tenant sinners—us. Earth is showing the wear and tear.
- We sinful human beings, all of us in all of time, have been hopelessly homesick for Eden. "Our ancestors were from Eden and something in us has never forgotten that."
- God intends to one day demolish this earth, literally melt it down, and start over.
- The climax of history will be new heavens and a New Earth, a redeemed and resurrected universe inhabited by a redeemed and resurrected people. "We will live on a planet so much like this one that it will be called the New Earth."
- The only way to gain title to this new home is through a personal relationship with the King of Heaven, Jesus Christ. "If you confess with your mouth Jesus as Lord, and believe in your heart that God raised Him from the dead, you will be saved."[21]
- Nurtured memories of the past form the baseline of our present identity and the foundation of our future. At no time is this more true than when we consider Christ's past sacrifice, our present identity in him, and our future home in heaven.

KEY QUESTIONS

1. Most importantly, have you accepted Christ as your personal Savior and Lord?
2. Have you allowed yourself to dream, thoughtfully, of your future with Jesus?

3. Can you imagine exploring a resurrected Eden or wandering through the magnificent vistas of a brand New Earth?

4. Do you anticipate meeting some of your ancestors who lived centuries before you on the future New Earth?

5. Can you envision future conversations with past heroes of the Bible?

6. Can you imagine your dreams fulfilled? Can you imagine rest, adventure, meaningful work, absolute personal joy, rich worship, and the deepest of friendships and interpersonal communion?

7. Can you imagine being completely, fully, and restfully at home, forever? The ultimate happily ever after—except this is reality, not a fairy tale.

MOVING FORWARD

Read *Heaven* by Randy Alcorn. Apart from the Bible itself, this book may be the most life-changing book you will ever read. Instead of trying to build your own dream home, live the rest of your life focused on God and the dream home he has prepared for you. I promise you, if you will take these truths to heart, they will improve the quality of your life. Forever.

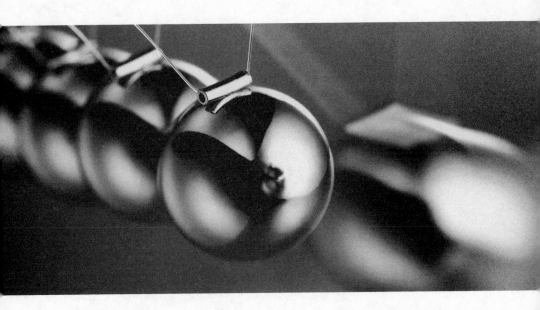

ALMOST MORNING

God has no beginning and no end. When the resurrected Son of God said, "I am the Alpha and the Omega, the beginning and the end,"[1] he was speaking of his relationship to the timeline.

Alpha . . . he was at the very beginning.

Omega . . . he will be at the very end.

In fact, he's at both ends right now. He is both the Ancient of Days and the Coming King. He is the Lamb slain from the foundation of the earth, and he is the Lamb that all of heaven will praise. He is the one "who is, and who was, and who is to come."[2]

Hebrews tells us that God is the "author and finisher of our faith."[3]

Author . . . our spiritual rebirth began with him. He was there when we started our race, cheering us on.

Finisher . . . one day every one of us will cross the finish line, and he will be there, urging us to finish strong and welcoming us home.

He is both the Alpha and the Omega of the timeline and the author and finisher of your (and my) two inches of the timeline. And he is everywhere in between.

You hem me in—behind and before;
you have laid your hand upon me.
Such knowledge is too wonderful for me,
too lofty for me to attain.[4]

Our little portions of the timeline may be very brief in comparison to the whole. Even so, when we find ourselves in the midst of serious life trials, the hours and days can seem to drag on and on.

You're worried about a son or daughter who should be home and in bed, and the hours of the night seem endless as you wait.

You're grieving a great loss, perhaps of a spouse or a child, and the heaviness it bears weighs down on you. You can hardly bear to think of what you imagine to be the empty years that stretch endlessly into an unknown future.

You find yourself all alone on a winter afternoon, and time seems to stand still as you endure the loneliness.

The Lord understands. He created us to live in time and to live in the person of the timeless Lord Jesus, who subjected himself to time's limitations and understands its dynamics. And after all, it won't really be all that long before the timeline reaches its terminus and the unimaginable splendor and joy of eternity begin for God's sons and daughters.

Facing torture, imprisonment, and likely constant pain from his many beatings, Paul wrote, "For our light affliction, which is but for a moment, is working for us a far more exceeding and eternal weight of glory."[5]

Speaking of the Lord's coming back for his own, the Bible says, "For in just a very little while, 'He who is coming will come and will not delay.'"[6]

The apostle John, who was actually permitted to look down the timeline into the future, had the distinct impression—even in his era—that the world as we know it would soon come to an end. He wrote, "The time is near."[7]

In the next to last verse in the Bible, the Lord himself says, "Yes, I am coming quickly."[8]

Concerning the sorrows of life, David reminds us, "Weeping may last for the night, but a shout of joy comes in the morning."[9]

God looks down on our little portions of the timeline and says to us, "I know the night is dark, and it seems like the weeping will never end. But truly . . . it's just for a night. Can you endure one night? The end isn't so far away. Your sorrow and disappointment are almost over.

"It's almost morning."

NOTES

Frontispiece
1. Frederick Buechner, *Telling Secrets* (New York: Harper Collins, 1991), 65–66.

Introduction: The Timeline
1. J. R. R. Tolkien, *The Hobbit,* revised edition (New York: Ballantine, 1966), 84.
2. Psalm 31:14–15, NIV
3. Ecclesiastes 3:11, NIV
4. Acts 17:26, NIV, emphasis added
5. Luke 12:25–26, NIV, emphasis added
6. Psalm 90:12, NIV
7. Romans 13:11, NLT

Chapter 1: Purpose and Power
1. C. S. Lewis, *The Screwtape Letters* (San Francisco: HarperCollins, 2001), 139.
2. James 4:14, THE MESSAGE
3. 2 Peter 3:8, NIV
4. Psalm 139:5, NLT
5. Colossians 2:13–14, NLT
6. Isaiah 1:18, NLT
7. Frederick Buechner, *Telling Secrets* (New York: HarperCollins, 1991), 32.

Chapter 2: Strengthening Your Future
1. Randy Alcorn, "School Shootings: Why?" Eternal Perspective Ministries, http://www.epm.org/articles/shootings.html.
2. Ibid.

3. Charles Swindoll, *Home, Where Life Makes Up Its Mind* (Portland, Ore.: Multnomah, 1979).

4. General Tommy Franks, *American Soldier* (New York: HarperCollins, 2004), xx.

5. Ibid., xx–xxi, 1.

6. Lynn Anderson, *Longing for a Homeland* (West Monroe, La.: Howard, 2004), 107–108. Song Lyrics are from "Home" by Joe Diffie, *16 Biggest Hits* (Sony, 2002).

7. Edgar Guest, "Home," from *A Heap o' Livin'* (New York: Lighthouse, 1916).

8. John Meacham, "Where Have All the Causes Gone?" *Newsweek,* January 27, 1997, 88.

Chapter 3: Springboard to Action

1. These remarks by Mrs. Reagan were quoted in *World* magazine, October 5, 2002.

2. Psalm 77:11–12; 78:5–7, NASB

3. John 14:26, NASB

4. Isaac Watts, *The Improvement of the Mind* (1798).

5. Deuteronomy 7:18, NIV

6. Exodus 2:24, NASB

7. Jeremiah 14:10, NASB

8. Philippians 1:27, NASB

9. See Revelation 20:11–15.

10. Genesis 3:1, NIV

11. Numbers 11:5, NASB, emphasis added

12. Deuteronomy 32:7, NASB

13. Deuteronomy 6:7, NASB

14. The phrase "ancient words, ever true" is from the song "Ancient Words," by Lynn DeShazo, ©2001, Integrity's Hosanna! Music.

15. Genesis 16:12, NIV

16. Read the story of Jacob's amazing wrestling match in Genesis 32:22–32.

17. 1 Timothy 4:8, NASB

18. Deuteronomy 8:2, 11, 18–19, NASB

19. Psalm 77:11–12; 78:5, 7, NASB

20. Jeremiah 6:16, NASB

21. Psalm 1:1-3, NIV
22. Job 8:8-10, NLT
23. Psalm 103:14, NIV
24. See 1 John 1:1.
25. 2 Peter 1:12-15, PHILLIPS, emphasis added

Chapter 4: Marking Today's Key Moments

1. Genesis 3:8, THE MESSAGE
2. Malachi 1:2, NLT; 11-13, THE MESSAGE
3. Malachi 3:16-17, NASB
4. George Santayana, *The Life of Reason* (Amherst, N.Y.: Prometheus, 1998), 82.
5. Larry Libby, "Treasures of the Heart," *Discipleship Journal,* Issue 139 (2004).
6. http://thewall-usa.com/information.asp
7. Joshua 4:7, NIV
8. Randy Alcorn, *Heaven* (Wheaton, Ill.: Tyndale, 2004), 17.
9. Ibid.
10. Dana Gioia, "Planting a Sequoia," in *The Gods of Winter* (St. Paul: Graywolf, 1991).

Chapter 5: Honoring Repeated Events

1. Jaroslav Pelikan, *The Vindication of Tradition: The 1983 Jefferson Lecture in the Humanities,* reprint edition (New Haven, Conn.: Yale University, 1986), 65.
2. Ibid., 81.
3. David Lowenthal, *The Heritage Crusade* (Cambridge, England: Cambridge University, 1998), 21.
4. See Exodus 12:15-20.
5. Exodus 12:14, NASB
6. 2 Timothy 3:14, NIV

Chapter 6: The Importance of Place

1. Genesis 2:8, NASB
2. Genesis 13:3-4, NIV
3. Genesis 35:6-7, NASB

4. 2 Peter 1:16-18, NLT

5. 2 Peter 1:19, NLT

6. Frederick Buechner, *The Longing for Home: Recollections and Reflections* (San Francisco: Harper, 1996), 4.

7. 2 Samuel 23:15, NKJV, emphasis added

8. 2 Samuel, 23:1, NKJV

9. Katherine Dalton, *Chronicles,* September 1997, 48.

10. Lynn Anderson, *Longing for a Homeland* (West Monroe, La.: Howard, 2004), 78.

11. Jennifer Rabin, "The Memory of a House," *Oregon Home,* November/ December 2003, 32.

12. Katherine Dalton, "Homegrown," *Chronicles,* September 1997, 46–48.

13. Snow Anderson, "My Turn," *Newsweek,* February 28, 2000, 10.

14. Ibid.

15. Jozef Glodek, "My Father's Gift," *The Plain Truth,* November/December 2001, 34–38.

Chapter 7: Trail Markers

1. 1 Samuel 7:2, NIV

2. 1 Samuel 7:8, NIV

3. 1 Samuel 7:10, NLT

4. 1 Samuel 7:12, NIV

Chapter 8: Why Are You Here?

1. John Dos Passos, *The Theme Is Freedom* (New York: Dodd, Mead, 1956), 159.

2. Acts 17:25-26, NIV

3. Psalm 139:1-5, 15, 16, NASB

4. Acts 17:26-27, NIV

Chapter 9: The Catapult

1. See 2 Kings 20:8-11.

2. Read the incredible true account in Joshua 10.

3. See John 11.

4. Jeremiah 1:5, NIV

5. Psalm 139:5, NKJV

6. Psalm 139:6, NKJV
7. Joel 2:25, AMP
8. Psalm 119:105, NASB
9. Isaiah 1:18, NASB
10. 1 Chronicles 1:11-12, NIV
11. 1 Chronicles 5:13-15, NASB
12. 1 Corinthians 15:22, NIV
13. Joni Eareckson Tada, "Dubious Roots," *Moody* magazine, March 1992, 34.
14. Acts 17:25-26, NIV, emphasis added
15. Psalm 139:3, 15-16, NASB

Chapter 10: Carving Your Name on the Timeline
1. Genesis 50:25, NASB
2. Sean McMeekin, "Grandma, Where Have You Gone?" *Boundless,* 2001:
   http://www.boundless.org/2001/features/a0000531.html.

Chapter 11: Start Right Here
1. Psalm 61:5, NIV, emphasis added
2. Hebrews 12:1, THE MESSAGE
3. Psalm 119:111, NIV, emphasis added
4. Psalm 27:10, NIV
5. Psalm 45:16-17, NIV
6. John 14:2-3, NLT
7. Hebrews 11:13-16, NASB
8. See Hebrews 13:8.
9. Revelation 21:4, NIV
10. "It Is No Secret," by Carl Stuart Hamblen
11. Stu Weber, *Tender Warrior* (Sisters, Ore.: Multnomah, 1999), 160.
12. Hebrews 11:1, NASB
13. Hebrews 11:6; 12:1-2, NASB
14. Hebrews 11:10, NASB
15. Romans 3:23, NIV
16. Romans 6:23, NIV
17. 1 Corinthians 15:3-4, NIV
18. Romans 10:9, NIV
19. Acts 4:12, NASB

20. Ephesians 2:8–9, NASB, emphasis added

21. Romans 10:13, NASB

22. After you've become a Christian, I'd strongly recommend a couple of key follow-up steps. First, get plugged in to a genuine New Testament church, one that takes God's Word seriously, takes itself seriously, and takes you seriously. Second, read! Read your Bible, and with some recommendations from your pastor, stop by your local Christian bookstore and pick up a few Christian classics for starters. Consume them.

Here are a few thoughts to help you appreciate your new heritage in Christ. Read carefully through Paul's letter to the Ephesians several times. Focus especially on chapter 2. The first ten verses describe what it means for you to be "resurrected with Christ," a new member of his family. Verses 11–22 describe "the new humanity," the new person you have become, and your new identity. It tells you something of the magnificent heritage that is now yours.

Once "dead in your trespasses and sins" (Ephesians 2:1, NASB), you are now quite alive. Forever. Once victimized by sin—your own and others—you are now free not to sin. You no longer have to walk in the dark world of your past. You don't have to follow "the course of this world" (v. 2). Once you were condemned because like every human being you were by nature "children of wrath" (v. 3). But God, "because of His great love" for you (v. 4), made you alive "together with Christ" (v. 5). And he did it so he could show you the "surpassing riches of His grace" (v. 7). This is purely a gift from God to you. He likes you! You didn't do anything to deserve his love; but he is a lover, and he loves *you*. He has made you his child!

Ephesians 2:11–22 describes something of the new family and heritage that you now enjoy. *Alienation* is not only a popular word in our world, but it is a fairly accurate description of our society. People are separated and isolated from one another and from God. People are disillusioned, critical, grumpy, and negative—not exactly healthy traits for getting along. Ephesians 2:12 uses the word *aliens* (NKJV) to describe what it's like to live without God.

Now that you've come to Christ, the old alienation you experienced is over! You're no longer *separate* or *excluded*. But you, once "far off" and a stranger, are now "brought near" (v. 13). You've been invited home by none other than the Son himself. He has brought you home and broken down any barriers between you and him (v. 14). You're at peace (v. 15). He has made you a member of the family forever!

This is not just a kingdom. It is a kingdom, but it's much more personal than that. It is truly the *"family"* you have always longed for. You are now a member "of God's household" (v. 19). You are now established "on the foundation of the apostles and prophets" (v. 20).

Chapter 12: Gaining Perspective

1. Genesis 15:1, NKJV
2. See 2 Kings 6:15–17.
3. Mark 8:24, NIV
4. 1 Corinthians 13:12, NIV
5. Genesis 15:5, NASB
6. Jeremiah 29:11, NIV
7. Romans 8:18–19, PHILLIPS
8. 1 John 3:2, NLT
9. Luke 12:32, NKJV
10. Genesis 15:7, NASB
11. Genesis 15:13–16, NASB
12. Revelation 1:8, 19, NASB
13. Revelation 4:6, 8, NIV, emphasis added
14. See James 1:5–8.

Chapter 13: The End Is Only the Beginning

1. Luke 7:13–15, NIV
2. John 10:28, NIV
3. John 17:24, NLT
4. Job 19:25–27, NKJV
5. Ephesians 2:2, NASB
6. Isaiah 6:3, NASB
7. Frederick Buechner, *Telling Secrets* (New York: HarperCollins, 1991), 65–66.
8. This quote is widely attributed to former U.S. Secretary of the Treasury Ivy Baker Priest.

9. 2 Peter 3:10, NASB
10. 2 Peter 3:5, 7, NASB
11. 2 Peter 3:13, NASB
12. Revelation 21:1, 3-4, NASB
13. Randy Alcorn, "True Thoughts about Heaven," Eternal Perspective Ministries, 2006. Article can be viewed at www.epm.org/articles/thoughts_heaven.html.
14. Lee Strobel, "Foreword" in Lynn Anderson, *Longing for a Homeland* (West Monroe, La.: Howard, 2004), ix, x.
15. Hebrews 11:13-14, 16, NASB
16. John 14:2, NASB
17. These quotations are from an unpublished draft of *Heaven* by Randy Alcorn, © 2004 by Randy Alcorn. All rights reserved. Used by permission.
18. Ibid.
19. Madeleine L'Engle, *Penguins and Golden Calves: Icons and Idols in Antarctica and Other Unexpected Places* (Colorado Springs: Shaw, 2003).
20. Annie Herring, "Goin' Home" (Myrrh, 1974).
21. Romans 10:9, NASB

Epilogue: Almost Morning
1. Revelation 21:6, NASB
2. Revelation 1:4, NIV
3. Hebrews 12:2, NKJV
4. Psalm 139:5-6, NIV
5. 2 Corinthians 4:17, NKJV
6. Hebrews 10:37, NIV
7. Revelation 1:3, NIV
8. Revelation 22:20, NASB
9. Psalm 30:5, NASB

ABOUT THE AUTHOR

Stu Weber graduated from Wheaton College and holds advanced degrees from Western Seminary. A U.S. Army veteran, he was awarded three bronze stars as a Green Beret in Vietnam. It was there, in the trauma and uncertainty of war, that Stu committed himself to a lifetime of vocational ministry. Stu is a pastor who loves his family, his country, and Christ's church.

More than thirty years ago, Stu and his wife, Linda, joined a small group of friends in founding Good Shepherd Community Church, a thriving Oregon church family, where they still worship and serve.

Stu is the author of a number of best-selling books, including *Tender Warrior, All the King's Men, Four Pillars of a Man's Heart,* and *Spirit Warriors.* He has also written the Matthew volume in the Holman New Testament Commentary series.

Stu and Linda live near Portland, Oregon, where they greatly enjoy their three grown sons, three wonderful "daughters-in-love," and seven grandchildren.

Also from Tyndale House Publishers

WE ALL HAVE QUESTIONS about what Heaven will be like. Now, in the most comprehensive book collection on Heaven to date, Randy Alcorn invites you to consider what the Bible says about Heaven. These books will help you to understand Heaven more deeply through study and will provide convenient information about eternity to those who are seeking answers.

- The foundational book, *Heaven*, contains all the details about Heaven and the New Earth given in the Bible. It also includes an extensive Q & A section in the second half of the book.

- *Heaven Study Guide* provides more than 250 thought-provoking questions, excerpts from *Heaven*, and Scripture references to guide your study.

- *Heaven: Biblical Answers to Common Questions* is a 64-page booklet that provides a sampling of some of the common questions about life after death addressed in the book *Heaven*. This is a great booklet for non-Christians (also available in packs of 20).